June 5th 2001

Dear Mike & Gill,

Thank you so much for your fantastic present. It is such an imaginative gift. We are thrilled with any excuse to go & have a picnic & you've provided the perfect means of enjoying those times even more. We are enclosing a small gift which we thought you might enjoy. It was stumbled upon in rather a strange manner & you may well enjoy that tale more than the book....

It was wonderful to share our wedding day with you, lots of love, Groover & so over to

Daniel →

P.O. BOX 402/BROOKLIN, ME/04616 USA

King's Manor Gallery, University of York,
Exhibition Square, York
YO1 2EP

ISBN 0 9520857 0 4

Cover illustration: Catalogue No. 24

Printed by Maxiprint, Colour Printers, York, England

CONTENTS

ACKNOWLEDGEMENTS

This exhibition of prints in my possession was originally organised at the invitation of Professor Jacques Berthoud of the Department of English and Related Literature at the University of York for the meeting of the 13th Triennial conference of the International Association of Professors of English held in York in 1986. Forty of the prints shown here were included, a typewritten catalogue was produced, and the exhibition was also seen at Wolfson College, Oxford, where I held the Michael Bromberg Fellowship for the study of prints 1981-3. This new showing has enabled a larger selection of prints to be exhibited. A grant from the Paul Mellon Centre for Studies in British Art has enabled an expanded catalogue to be printed and thus make available illustrations of some little-known literary prints; I am very grateful to Professor Michael Kitson and his Advisory Board.

The University of York has provided generous support from its Art Committee and from the F. R. Leavis Fund, which is administered through the Department of English. Further support has come from the Provost of Langwith College, as well as from the Provosts of Alcuin, Derwent, Goodricke and Vanbrugh Colleges, all at the University of York.

Thanks are also due to Alexandra Parigoris, of the University of York, who is responsible for the University's Art Gallery in the King's Manor, for making arrangements for the exhibition to be shown and the catalogue to be printed, to David Whiteley, the University photographer for taking all the photographs, and to my wife Helena Moore for her help and encouragement.

The catalogue is being sold in aid of the Laurence Sterne Trust, which owns Laurence Sterne's last home, Shandy Hall, some 20 miles north of York, and the exhibition is available for further showings in order to promote sales of the publication. The Trust is mounting an appeal to create an endowment to safeguard the future of the house, which is open to the public on Wednesday and Sunday afternoons in the summer or by appointment with the Hon. Curator, Shandy Hall, Coxwold, York Y06 4AD. Shandy Hall has established itself as a home for Sterne studies; a scholarly annual, The *Shandean,* was launched in 1989 and links have been forged with the English Department of the University of York.

David Alexander, December 1992

INTRODUCTION

The aim of this exhibition is to show some of the prints of English literature engraved in the last quarter of the eighteenth century which were singly issued rather than being in books. Most of these are in the technique of stipple, which suddenly became popular with the increased demand for decorative prints in the 1770s. Such prints were usually bought as 'furniture', that is to be framed - often in elegant gilt circles or ovals - and displayed on the wall rather than being kept in albums and portfolios. It was the great expansion of the English print market at this time, coinciding with an increase in the public appetite for literature, which encouraged artists to paint or draw scenes from literature. In the 1780s several publishers, notably James Birchall, J.R.Smith and Thomas Macklin, issued considerable numbers of prints of English literature, and their success encouraged Macklin and John Boydell to open separate galleries where they exhibited pictures commissioned from the leading painters of the day. The scale of these later undertakings inevitably led to uneven results; nevertheless the literary prints of this period are interesting for a number of reasons. Many of them are not merely by-products of paintings, as are most prints, since the pictures on which they are based were conceived in order to be engraved. They are an indication of the contemporary popularity of different writers, many of them forgotten today, and of how people interpreted them. Finally they include some of the most attractive of English colour prints, made at a time when engraving on copper was at its best, and many of these can give pleasure whether or not the viewer has any knowledge of their literary connections.

On the whole artists looked for moving incidents to depict - hence the 'Affecting Moments' title of this exhibition; a very high proportion of the prints show female emotion, frequently distress, treated in a sentimental way, but not all artists succumbed to the fashion for sentimentality, as the selection of prints after Henry Fuseli makes clear.

British artists and literature before 1775

England had a small but flourishing school of book illustration from the early eighteenth century. There were specialist illustrators, notably Hubert Gravelot (1699-1773), but many painters such as Francis Hayman (1708-76) produced drawings for the publishers. There were successsive illustrated editions of Shakespeare's plays, and many other works appeared with illustrations, or at least decorative frontispieces. It should be emphasised that works of imaginative literature seldom appeared initially with plates. Although some authors took a passing interest in illustrations to their books - for example Laurence Sterne flattered William Hogarth into providing frontispieces for volumes II and IV of the second edition of his novel *Tristram Shandy* in 1760 - there was little of the creative collaboration between illustrators and authors of imaginative works seen after 1835, when much fiction first appeared in illustrated parts. Most eighteenth century plates were commissioned by publishers to add interest to new editions of the classics or reissues of popular works by living authors.

Before 1760 there were relatively few paintings or singly issued prints of English literature, partly because English collectors were not interested in such pictures and would generally only buy subject pictures from the continent. Hogarth demonstrated that painters could, in theory, free themselves from total reliance on portrait painting by publishing prints of other kinds of pictures. The market for prints of decorative genre pictures - for example mezzotints after Philip Mercier (1689-1760) - certainly flourished and there was also a market for prints of historical interest appealing to English patriotism, especially after the translation of Paul de Rapin-Thoyras's *History of England,* 1743-47, which highlighted many of the dramatic incidents which were picked on by painters for the next 150 years[1]. At this time, however, few painters turned to native literature. One exception was Hayman, who painted some literary pictures, which were engraved, for the decoration of a place of entertainment, Vauxhall Gardens [2] Another was Joseph Highmore (1692-1780), who in 1744 published a set of prints of *Pamela,* the improving novel by Samuel Richardson (1689-1761) which had just been published; these were based on his set of twelve paintings (now divided between the Tate Gallery, the Fitzwilliam Museum, and the National Gallery of Victoria, Melbourne). Most painters had no choice but to paint portraits until after 1760; it then became easier to paint uncommissioned pictures since they might find buyers in the public exhibitions, at the Society of Artists from 1760 and at the Royal Academy from 1769. Exhibitions greatly helped the careers of those, such as Benjamin West (1738-1820) and Joseph Wright of Derby (1734-97), who aimed to paint various kinds of historical picture; their pictures became widely known through the tonal process of mezzotint and later also through line engraving, which was considered the appropriate medium for history painting. The best known line engraving of the 1760s was the print commissioned by the publisher John Boydell (1719-1804) and engraved by William Woollett (1735-85) after the landscape by Richard Wilson exhibited in 1760 showing a story from classical mythology, *The Destruction of the Children of Niobe.* The success of this print established Boydell as a major force in print publishing for forty years.[3] Five years later Wilson exhibited a painting showing the tragic story of Celadon's loss of his beloved Amelia, struck by lightning as they walked in the countryside, as related in *The Seasons* by James Thomson (1700-48); this was engraved by Woollett in 1766. As David Solkin has commented it could be said that in this subject Wilson 'found a modern, English, and Christian equivalent to the..."Niobe" '. The four seasons had of course long been a stock subject for painters and Thomson's verses were subsequently attached to many prints based on pictures which had been painted without the poem in mind; however as has been pointed out, not only was the poem particularly admired for its pictorial qualities, Thomson had praised famous painters such as Claude and Rosa, implicitly presenting a challenge to contemporary artists. [4]

Kauffman's literary pictures

The painter who made most use of literary subjects was Angelica Kauffman, who arrived in England in 1766, well-read and fluent in several languages. At first she drew on classical stories but later she depicted scenes from British literature, often for the print trade. In 1773 she exhibited at the Royal Academy a painting based on an incident in Ossian - thought at the time to be a genuine Celtic poet rather than the invention of the 'translator' James Macpherson. [5] This was engraved in mezzotint by Thomas Burke (1749-1815) and published the same year by William Wynne Ryland (1733-83) as *Inibaca discovering herself to Trenmor.* It was the following year that the first stipple engravings began to appear; this technique, which used patterns of etched or engraved dots to build up areas of tone, saw the emergence of a more delicate kind of engraving, better suited to the demand for elegant 'furniture' prints, and capable of printing larger numbers of impressions than mezzotint, since mezzotint plates wore quickly and had to be reworked. Stipple plates also had the advantage that they could be more easily printed in colours; this was a laborious exercise which involved printing *à la poupée,* that is dabbing the different colours onto the plate for each printing; such prints were usually double the price of those in a single colour. Printing in colour did however produce much finer effects than colouring prints with watercolour. A simpler way of making stipples more decorative was to print them in shades of sanguine or sepia.

Between 1774 and his death in 1784 Ryland published over thirty stipples after Kauffman; only a few - *Patience,* published 1777, from *Caractacus,* a poem by William Mason (1724-97), *Maria,* published 1779, from Sterne (No. 38) and its pendant *Eloisa,* from Pope - were clearly based on English literature, though Kauffman's self-portrait as *Hope,* published in 1775, bears verses from Pope. The first two were among only three pictures of English literature which Kauffman exhibited at the Royal Academy. The tragic figure of Maria was one which made an enormous impact; prints of her work were exported in large numbers, many were copied by continental engravers, and this image in particular became very well-known. [6]

Publishers of literary stipples

Print publishers began to seek suitable pictures which could be turned into stipple furniture prints, and several portraits were transformed in this way. The first picture by Joshua Reynolds (1723-92) to receive this treatment was his portrait of his niece Theophila Palmer reading Clarissa Harlowe, which was engraved as an oval stipple by a young Russian engraver working in London, Gabriel Scoromodoff (1752-92) and published by V.M.Picot in 1775 (Fig. 1). It was published initially without a title, but was reissued by Boydell as

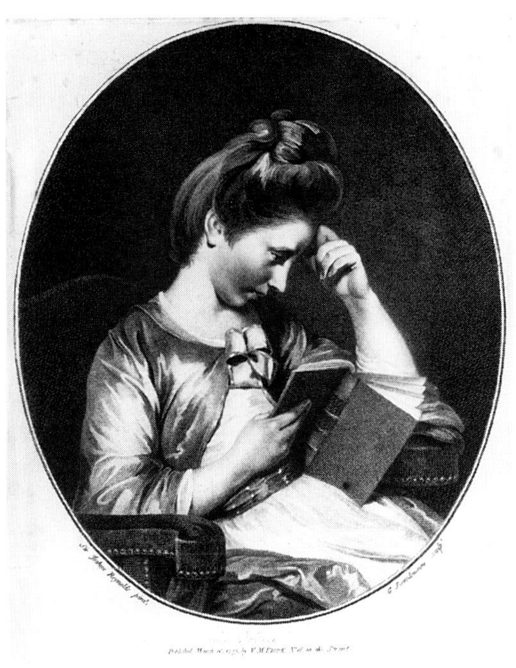

Figure 1

Reflections on Clarissa Harlowe in 1785. This print symbolises, as it were, the increased interest which women were showing in literature; they were also becoming more important as buyers of prints and the rage for stipples reflected the penetration of quickly changing fashions into the print market.

Portraits did not generally carry the emotional weight which publishers needed in order to produce prints which would appeal to heightened sensibilities. It was not until the 1780s that stipples of literary subjects began to appear in large numbers. Thus John Raphael Smith (1752-1812), the finest mezzotint engraver of his time, who began publishing prints in 1772, did not begin issuing stipples until 1781. Throughout his career he engraved many literary pictures in mezzotint, starting with The Bard, from *Mr Gray's Ode...founded on a Tradition ...that Edward 1st...order'd all the Bards.. to be put to Death,* engraved and exhibited at the Society of Artists in 1775 after the picture shown there the previous year. [7] In 1775 he also produced a set of four prints of touching incidents in *The Sentimental Journey* by Laurence Sterne (1713-68); this had been published in 1768 and its succession of sentimental encounters made it immediately popular; it soon became clear which incidents were most suited to illustration, both in the book and in separately issued prints and the selection seldom varied. [8]

Smith also engraved six mezzotints after pictures by Henry Fuseli, including his *Lear and Cordelia* (No. 4). Fuseli was the best-read of all painters then working in England, and had been making drawings of scenes from English literature from the time he was a student in Rome. [9] Given the importance of mezzotint for reproducing literary pictures a small group, mostly by Smith, is shown as the first section of this exhibition. During the 1780s and 1790s Smith engraved or published a great number of literary subjects by other painters as varied as William Beechey (1753-1839), James Northcote (1746-1831) and George Morland.(1763-1804), and he attached literary tags to prints after other painters such as Reynolds (No. 13). On occasion it was a contemporary picture which inspired literature rather than vice versa; Fuseli's *Nightmare* - a product of his interest in witchcraft - inspired verses by Erasmus Darwin (1731-1802) which were engraved below the print which Smith issued (No. 6) some years before they were formally published.

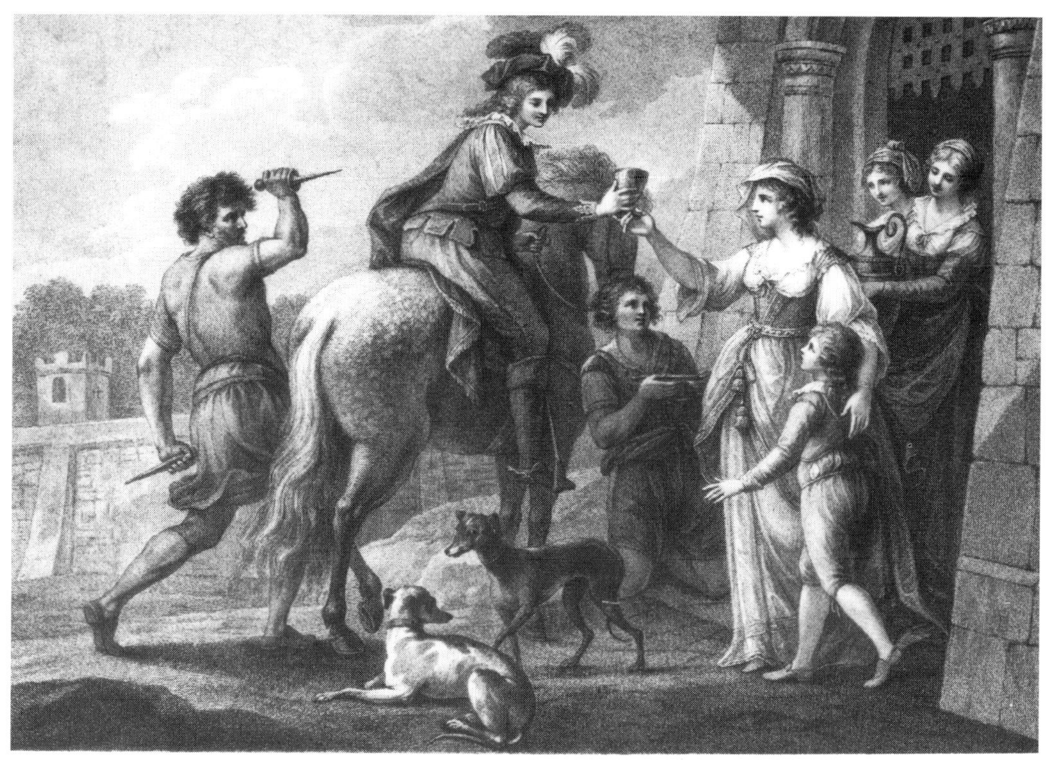

Figure 2

It is not clear how many of the pictures which Smith engraved had been bought or commissioned by him. There is clear evidence however of the extent to which another publisher active in the 1780s had been the owner of many of the pictures he had engraved. James Birchall (d. 1794), who was a carver and gilder by profession and not an engraver, began publishing prints of literary subjects in the early 1780s; when his stock was sold in 1795 it included 43 pictures and 43 drawings, and it seems that he had owned other pictures which were not in this sale. [10] Of the pictures 18 were by William Hamilton (1751-1801); some of his paintings and drawings were for a series of prints of English history. Scenes from actual or imagined English history were an important source for affecting scenes and to reinforce this point one of *Edward the Martyr* after a drawing by Hamilton engraved for Birchall by Francesco Bartolozzi (1725-1815), who succeeded Ryland as the most important stipple engraver, is shown here (Fig. 2). Among the drawings owned by Birchall were six by the young German artist Henry Ramberg (1763-1840), including a pair illustrating Goldsmith's *Vicar of Wakefield* (Nos 42-3) [11] It is likely that many of these purchases had been commissions; it is known for example that Birchall bought four pictures of Shakespearian scenes from Kauffman - only two of which were in his sale - which she sent back from Rome in 1782, and which were engraved by Bartolozzi and by his best pupil Peltro Tomkins, both of whom tried their hands at designing literary prints (Nos 23,49). [12]

A new elegance in book illustration

At the same time that singly issued prints of English literature were becoming more popular, public expectation of book illustration was changing. [13] This was to a large measure due to the publisher John Bell (1745-1831), who took pride in improving the appearance of his widely sold books. [14] In 1778 he launched a series of miniature volumes of *The Poets of Great Britain,* followed by *Shakespeare* and by *British Drama,* beautifully printed and with very well engraved illustrations by leading artists of the day, including Kauffman, Philip de Loutherbourg (1740-1812), John Hamilton Mortimer (1741-79) and Francis Wheatley (1727-1801). These were painters rather than illustrators; two younger men, Edward Burney (1760-1848) and Thomas Stothard (1755-1834), found sufficient employment to specialise as illustrators. [15] Stothard began his career providing drawings for magazines, notably those published by John Harrison, who reprinted many classics in, for example, *The Novelist's Magazine.* Periodicals, together with frequently reprinted anthologies such as *The Beauties of Sterne,* 1782, and Vicesmus Knox's *Elegant Extracts,* 1783, did much to spread interest in literature and circulated very widely in the provinces. [16] Stothard also provided many designs for singly issued prints, a few of which he published himself with the engraver Edmund Scott (No. 5). [17]

Pine's Shakespearian venture

Stothard was one of many artists who tried, on occasion, to by-pass the print publishers by issuing prints after their own pictures, just as Hogarth had done. In 1781 the painter Robert Edge Pine announced that he was painting a series of Shakespearian scenes, of which he would publish prints in pairs 'till a set is obtained, which will sufficiently illustrate the first of Dramatic Poets'. In newspaper advertisements, headed 'Historical Painting' to emphasise the seriousness of the scheme, he suggested that Shakespeare

> *of all writers, claims the attention of the Historic Painter. These subjects, having hitherto been unattended to, but for frontispieces to the plays; it may be proper to observe, that the pictures proposed, are not meant to be representations of stage scenes, but will be treated with the more unconfined liberty of painting, in order to bring those images to the eye, which the writer has given to the mind; and which, in some instances, is not within the power of the Theatre.*

In 1782 Pine showed six of the paintings in a special exhibition, but after publishing a few prints engraved by Caroline Watson - the first woman engraver to work as an independent engraver in England - he sold the plates to Boydell (No. 56). As has been noted above Birchall was also publishing prints of Shakespearian scenes at this time; so was Thomas Macklin, another carver and gilder, who had begun to publish in 1780; from the start a high proportion of his prints were after literary subjects, which by 1785 had included Fielding, Hull, Ossian, Dryden, Spencer, Percy - not to mention Aristo, Tasso and Goethe's *Werther* - as well as depictions of Shakespeare by Fuseli and Stothard (No. 58).

Macklin's 'Poets Gallery'

It was Macklin who was the first publisher to have the confidence to change from ad hoc publishing of individual prints based on pictures that were generally borrowed or bought from the artist after they had been painted to a more ambitious and planned programme based on commissioned pictures. [18] In 1788 he announced a plan to publish *A Series of Prints illustrative of the most celebrated British Poets...with explanatory letter press.* He intended to issue one hundred large prints, at the rate of eight a year, after specially commissioned pictures, which were exhibited at his 'Poets Gallery' in Fleet Street, a good location since it was between the City and Westminster. In the event only 24 prints were issued before the changed economic climate, following the outbreak of war with France in 1793, obliged Macklin to end the venture. He was not able to commission paintings by Gainsborough and Reynolds, and had instead to use existing pictures; Reynolds's portrait group of Macklin's wife and a daughter was engraved by Bartolozzi as an illustration to Thomson's *Autumn* (Fig. 3). The poems illustrated included old favourites such as Edmund Spenser's *Faerie Queen* (No. 29), Oliver Goldsmith's *Deserted Village* (No. 31) and Thomas Gray's *Elegy* (No. 33) together with a few by living poets such as Edward Jerningham (No. 30). The principal painters were Fuseli and Hamilton, who both produced some fine paintings, and the pictures were well engraved in stipple, mostly by Bartolozzi and Tomkins. Macklin had other projects, notably a great

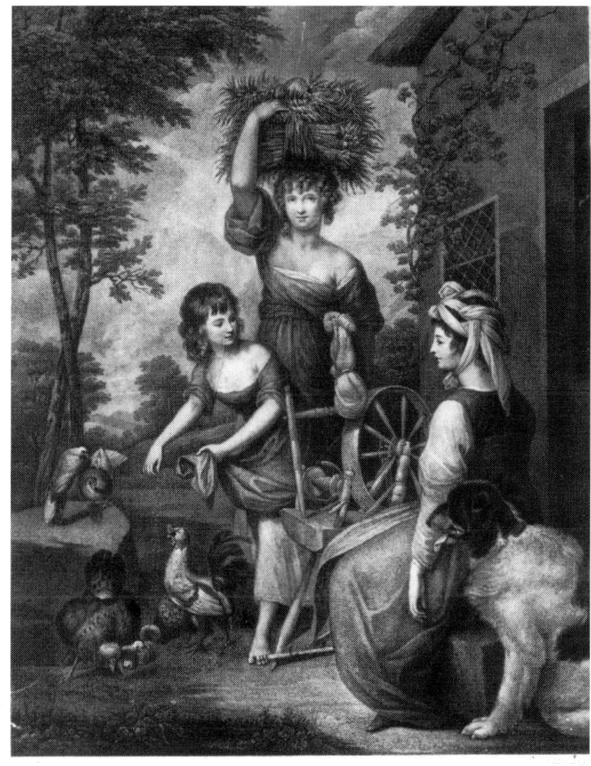

Figure 3

illustrated Bible, and he also continued to issue other prints, including a light-hearted series of Shakespearian scenes (No. 65) after designs by the fashionable amateur Henry Bunbury, whose portrait by the young Thomas Lawrence was engraved in 1787 and was often bought as a frontispiece to albums of his prints (Fig. 4). [19]

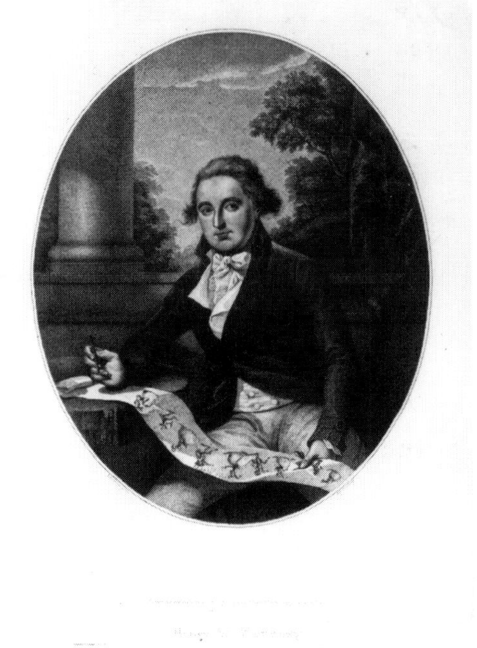

Figure 4

Boydell's *Shakespeare*

The most ambitious of all the projects was Boydell's *Shakespeare;* in 1786 he launched a subscription for an illustrated edition of the plays in imperial folio size. He managed to involve most of the leading painters and engravers in the scheme, announcing in a prospectus of May 1789 that 'the principal cause of the present undertaking' was to correct the neglect of historical painting; he made no mention of Pine's scheme, which may have helped to put the idea into his head. The paintings which he commissioned were exhibited at a special gallery, 'The Shakespeare Gallery' in Pall Mall, rather than in his shop in the City, and this became a fashionable meeting-place. Indeed the prospects for the venture seemed promising enough for a Dublin stationer, James Woodmason, to launch a Shakespeare Gallery in Ireland, commissioning pictures from many of the artists employed by Boydell; when this did not look like being a success Woodmason moved his pictures in 1794 to a 'New Shakespeare Gallery' near Boydell's Gallery in Pall Mall. [20]

Large plates of Boydell's pictures, a few in line but most in stipple, began to appear in 1791, but it was not until 1802 that the nine volume edition was complete. It had soon become clear that the hundred imperial folio plates were too large to serve as book illustrations; they came out in parts and were also issued without text in two volumes; another edition set of smaller prints, many after additional pictures, were engraved to serve as book illustrations. This meant considerable extra expense; the project was subject to great delays and the standard of some of the paintings and engravings came under criticism. It was certainly an achievement to have turned the attention of so many artists to literary illustration, but the scheme ultimately failed as much because of its artistic weaknesses as from the collapse of the export trade. [21] There were some well-received contributions, for example those of Northcote (No. 59) and the charming pictures of Matthew William Peters (1741/2-1814) (No. 60). As to be expected, the pictures provided by Fuseli are remarkable productions, in which he shows his relish for the sublime and the chilling (No.62). He threw most of his energies into these pictures between 1786 and 1789; in 1790 he decided to open his own 'Milton Gallery' with pictures painted exclusively by himself and so profit from the sale of engravings (No. 36) and this took up much of his time. [22] It is not clear exactly how work on the Shakespeare was allocated, but as Fuseli was one of the initial contributors he may have had his choice of subjects. Another early contributor was Kauffman, settled in Rome, to whom Boydell wrote; he probably sent her a list of the incidents already selected, leaving her a free choice of unchosen scenes; she wrote back at the end of 1787, apologising for her delay in replying to his letter and telling him that 'the subjects fixed on is for the one Troilus & Cressida.'(No. 63) 'the other Valentin rescuing Silvia from Protheus from the two Gentlemen of Verona'. [23]

The end of the fashion

Neither of Kauffman's pictures were particularly distinguished; the same could be said for too many of the contributions. Subscribers began to fall away and although the project was not abandoned it brought financial ruin to Boydell's firm. Boydell eventually claimed to have spent £300,000 on the venture; shortly before his death in 1804 he had to dispose of the Gallery by lottery, which brought £45,000, but the sale of the pictures only raised £6,000, which reflected the general judgement of them. A wider change in public opinion had taken place since the late 1780s. Something of a reaction had set in against the insipidity and superficiality of much contemporary painting - and indeed of literature. To a large extent it was the French Revolution and the tremendous threat it posed to the life of the monied and leisured purchasers of prints of 'affecting moments' which changed people's attitudes. Just as Hannah More, a critic of the cult of sensibility from the time of her *Essays..for Young Ladies* of 1777, looked back on her frivolous early years so others realised that what had moved them in their youth now seemed rather absurd. Lady Louisa Stuart read *The Man of Feeling,* the novel by an enthusiastic disciple of Sterne, Henry Mackenzie, on its publication in 1771. She later admitted that 'as I was a girl of fourteen not yet versed in sentiment, I had a secret dread I should not cry enough to gain the credit of proper sensibility'; fifty years later the company laughed when it was read aloud. In a similar way the sentimental prints of the time seemed rather ludicrous and were removed from the walls.

References

1 Roy Strong: *And when did you last see your father?,* London, 1978; although this is sub-titled *The Victorian Painter and British History* it also contains interesting information about eighteenth century painting.
2 Brian Allen, *Francis Hayman,* exhibition catalogue, London and New Haven, 1987.
3 Hermann A. Bruntjen, *John Boydell,* PhD. thesis, Stanford University, Ann Arbor, 1979.

4 David Solkin: *Richard Wilson,* exhibition catalogue, London,1982, p.221.

5 Kauffman, pl. 30.

6 For the large number of English prints after Kauffman see the chronological checklist in Kauffman.

7 Ellis Waterhouse, *Dictionary of British 18th Century Painters*, Woodbridge, 1981, illustrates the painting, p. 197.

8 see Catherine Gordon,' "More than one handle": the Development of Sterne Illustration 1760-1820', *Words: Wai-te-Ata Studies in Literature,* iv, Wellington, N.Z, 1974.

9 Nancy Pressly, *The Fuseli Circle in Rome,* exhibition catalogue, New Haven, 1979.

10 *Catalogue of...engraved copper plates...late the property of Mr James Birchall,* auction catalogue, Mrs Hutchins, 20-24 May 1795.

11 Ramberg is best known as a satirical artist (see the study by F.Forster-Hahn, Hanover, 1965).

12 See V.Manners and G.C.Williamson, *Angelica Kauffmann,* London, 1924 pp. 141-74 for a list of later paintings, including ones she sent back to England.

13 see Hammellmann for the development of book illustration.

14 Stanley Morison, *John Bell,* London 1930.

15 For Stothard see Coxhead; Shelley M.Bennett *Thomas Stothard: The Mechanisms of Art Patronage in England circa 1800, Columbia, Miss.,1988* does not cover Stothard's singly issued prints.

16 R.D.Mayo, *The English Novel in the Magazines,* Oxford, 1962.

17 for Scott see *The Scott Family at Home,* exhibition catalogue, Hove, 1988

18 T.S.R.Boase, 'Macklin and Bowyer', *Journal of the Warburg and Courtauld Institutes,* xxvi, 1963, pp. 148-177; Robert Bowyer opened his 'Historic Gallery' to show pictures for his illustrated edition of David Hume's *History of England.*

19 John Riely, *Henry William Bunbury,* exhibition catalogue, Sudbury, 1983.

20 Robin Hamlyn, 'An Irish Shakespeare Gallery', *Burlington Magazine,* cxx, 1978, pp. 515-529.

21 Winifred H.Friedmann, *Boydell's Shakespeare Gallery*, New York, 1976; all the prints are reproduced in intro. A.E.Santaniello, *The Boydell Shakespeare Prints,* Arno Press, New York, 1979.

22 For the 'Milton Gallery' see Schiff, Weinglass, and the catalogue of the Fuseli exhibition at the Tate Gallery, 1975.

23 Letter from Kauffman to Boydell dated 29 September 1787, Anderton Royal Academy Catalogues, 1289, British Museum Print Room.

CATALOGUE

The exhibition is divided into four sections: the first shows a few mezzotints; the second shows prints inspired by poetry; the third those inspired by novels, and the last prints of Shakespeare's plays. The prints are catalogued in chronological order, except those from Macklin's 'Poets Gallery' and Boydell's 'Shakespeare Gallery' which are grouped together.

Dimensions, in millimetres, height before width, are of platemarks; (those of the engraved area or 'subject' are given in brackets).

SECTION I: 1- 5 THE LITERARY MEZZOTINT

1. NAMPONT
Mezzotint by Valentine Green published by John Boydell, 1774, after a painting by George Carter exhibited at the Society of Artists, 1773, illustrating Sterne's *Sentimental Journey,* 1768.
Lit: Altick pl. 8
XXX

This print shows an old man whom Yorick sees at an inn door at Nampont. His ass, the friend who has accompanied him on a pilgrimage to Spain, has just died:

> *He then took his crust of bread out of his wallet again, as if to eat it; held it some time in his hand, then laid it upon the bit of his ass's bridle - looked wistfully at the little arrangement he had made, and then gave a sigh.*

George Carter (1737-94) was a painter of weak genre and historical pictures, several of which became known through prints which Carter arranged to have engraved. In 1785 he held an unsuccessful exhibition in London of thirty-five paintings, mostly of recent historical events but also including *Children's Games* inspired by a poem by William Shenstone.

Valentine Green (1739-1813) was one of the ablest of English mezzotint engravers; he was certainly the most ambitious and was a constant supporter of the cause of history painting. A very high proportion of his prints were of subject pictures rather than portraits; in 1775 he also engraved *The Cave of Despair,* illustrating Spenser's *Faerie Queen,* which was painted by Benjamin West, many of whose pictures Green engraved.

John Boydell (1719-1804) was the most ambitious and celebrated of print publishers in eighteenth century England, though his importance has been exaggerated. In 1769 he began to publish *A Collection of Prints, Engraved after the Most Capital Paintings in England,* which were principally line engravings of old master pictures. He published a number of literary mezzotints but at first he stood rather aloof from the fashion for stipple engravings; later he published several (Nos 21,45,47,48) but his inclination was towards grander prints, hence the large size of the prints issued from his 'Shakespeare Gallery' initiated in 1786 (Nos 59-63).

2. THE SWORD, RENNES

Mezzotint engraved and published by John Raphael Smith, 1775, after a painting by A.V.Rymsdyk exhibited at the Royal Academy, 1775, illustrating Sterne's *Sentimental Journey.*
Lit: Frankau 341, as after Carter
(subject, oval 285 x 240)

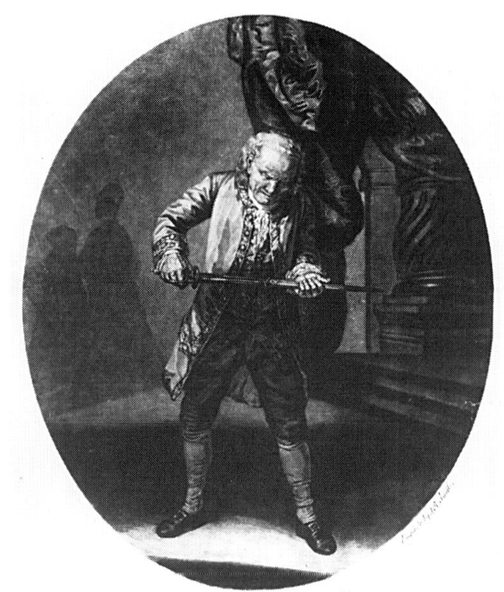

The Sword, Rennes

This print shows the touching moment when the Marquis d'E**, who had relinquished his nobility for many years in order to enter trade and repair the family fortune, reclaims his sword. He sheds a tear as he draws it almost out of the scabbard and notices a patch of rust. Yorick witnesses the scene: 'O how I envied him his feelings'.

Andreas van Rymsdyk (1754-86) was primarily a portrait painter. This early subject picture was engraved as one of a set of four mezzotints with three other prints after Carter, inspired by *The Sentimental Journey: The Captive, The Peasant* and *Le Patissier.*

John Raphael Smith (1752-1812) was the finest artist among English mezzotint engravers and gave great charm to many of the prints he engraved. He designed many prints himself, including a number of stipples. He became a successful publisher, notably of the rustic genre pictures painted by George Morland, but even so skilled and experienced an engraver as Smith found the economic difficulties brought by the war with France too difficult and in his last years he worked primarily as a painter of pastel portraits in the north of England.

3. SERENA

Mezzotint engraved and published by J.R.Smith, 1782, after a painting by George Romney illustrating William Hayley's poem *The Triumphs of Temper,* 1781.
Lit: Frankau 312
510 x 353 (475 x353)

This picture is a portrait of Honora Sneyd, later the second wife of Richard Lovell Edgeworth, painted as Serena, heroine of Hayley's poem. The poem and the print are a dual tribute to the success of Fanny Burney's novel *Evelina,* published in 1778, which Serena is reading. New works of literature were seldom provided with book illustrations and this print preceded the first illustrated Evelina of 1787, which has a plate after Thomas Stothard showing Serena in a very similar pose.

The print is a reminder - should one be necessary - that women were becoming more important both as readers and writers of imaginative works. There had of course been plenty of women authors before Fanny Burney, but the extraordinary success of this anonymous novel, which turned out to have been written by a very young woman from a well-known family, certainly gave female authorship added respectability.

George Romney (1734-1802) was thought by many to be in the same rank as Reynolds and Gainsborough at the time he painted this picture. He is remembered principally for his pictures of Emma Hart, who became Lady Hamilton in 1791. One of his major patrons was the poet William Hayley (see Nos 14-15).

4. LEAR AND CORDELIA

Mezzotint engraved and published by J.R.Smith, 1784, after a painting by Henry Fuseli, illustrating Shakespeare's *King Lear,* Act IV.
Lit: Frankau 212
450 x 553 (438 x 553)

This print shows Cordelia asking her father whether he knows her and being answered 'You are a spirit, I know'. Fuseli later painted a powerful picture of the

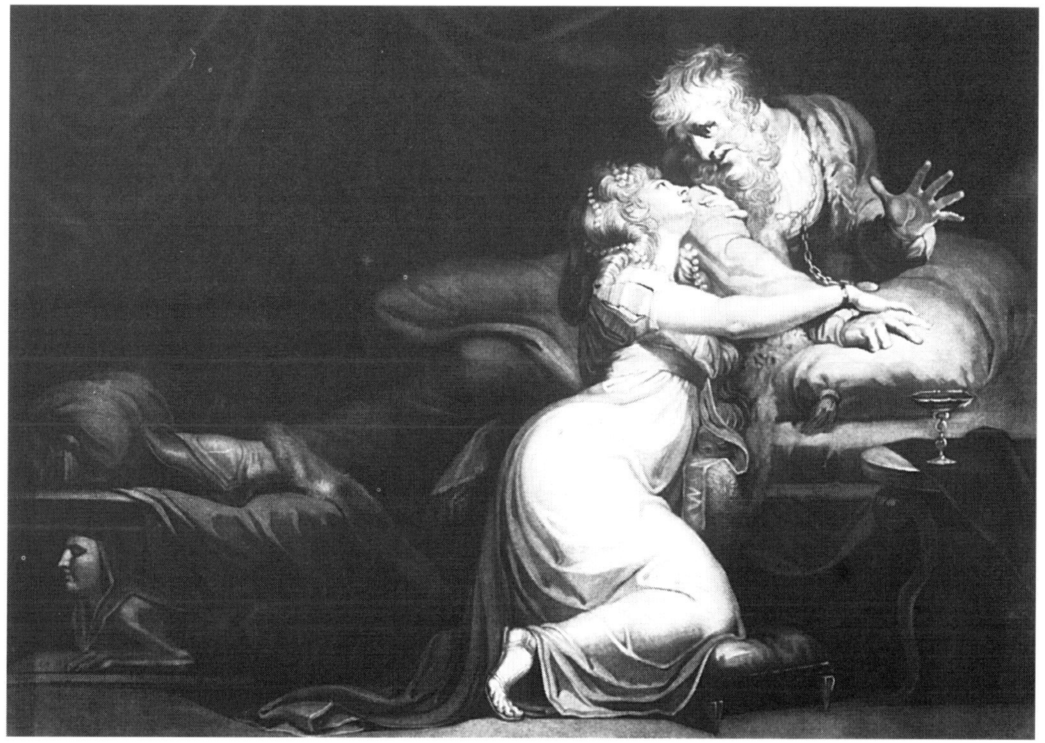

Lear and Cordelia

scene of *Lear dismissing Cordelia,* with which the play opens, for Boydell's Shakespeare Gallery.

Henry Fuseli (1741-1825) was born in Zurich, son of a writer on art. He was trained for the Zwinglian ministry and was ordained in 1761, but had to leave Zurich on account of his views. He was a man of great intellectual and literary attainments, with an early and enduring enthusiasm for classical and northern mythology, Shakespeare and Milton. He was also attracted to painting and it was the encouragement of Joshua Reynolds, whom he met in England in 1768, which persuaded him to opt for painting as a career. From 1770 to 1778 he studied in Rome, where his powerful personality and aggressive draughtsmanship inspired various British students there, such as Alexander Runciman (1736-85) and James Northcote, to take greater interest in depicting scenes from literature. He settled in London in 1778 and in the early 1780s five of his literary pictures were engraved in mezzotint by Smith, who was the publisher of a stipple of his most famous picture, *The Nightmare* (No. 6).

SECTION II : 5-37 SINGLY ISSUED PRINTS OF NOVELS

5. AULD ROBIN GRAY
Stipple by Edmund and Mary Ann Scott, published by Thomas Stothard and Edmund Scott, April 1782, after a painting by Stothard illustrating Lady Anne Lindsay's ballad of *Auld Robin Gray,* 1772.
232 x 268 (oval 190 x 238)

This popular ballad, which was depicted by various artists, tells how, in order to support her aged parents, the young Jenny submissively marries Auld Robin rather than wait for the return of her true love, who is away at sea. The anonymous Scottish ballad soon became widely known, in part because of the increased interest in northern ballads following the publication of Percy's *Reliques* in 1775. It was written by Lady Anne Lindsay, later Barnard, a daughter of the Earl of Balcarres, who did not publicly acknowledge her authorship for some years; she wrote the piece when she was 22, setting the words to an old tune 'to give its plaintive tones some little history of virtuous distress in humble life'.

This print was engraved by Edmund Scott (c. 1746-c.1810) and his wife Mary Ann, who signed a few prints as 'M.A.Rigg' before her marriage; it seems likely that she had learned to engrave from her fiancé as it was very difficult for girls to be apprenticed to engravers. Scott was a friend of Stothard, who was godfather to one of his sons, and also engraved his *Children in the Wood*, inspired by the melancholy ballad included in Percy's *Reliques* (ill. Coxhead, opp. p. 170). When stipple engravers found difficulty in getting employment in the 1790s Scott worked as a portrait draughtsman.

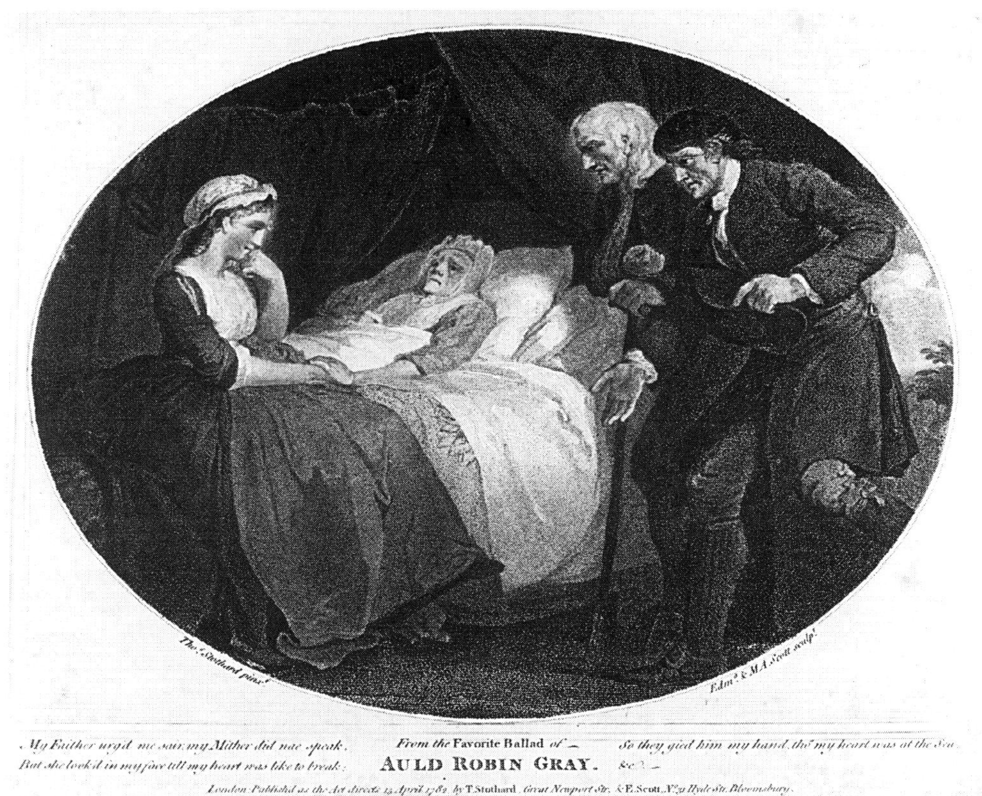

Auld Robin Grey

6 THE NIGHTMARE

Stipple by Thomas Burke, published by J.R.Smith, 30 January 1783, after the painting by Fuseli exhibited at the Royal Academy 1782, and now in the Detroit Institute of Arts.

Lit: Nicolas Powell, *Fuseli: The Nightmare,* London, 1973; John F.Moffitt, 'Malleus Maleficarum: A Literary Context for Fuseli's Nightmare', *Gazette des Beaux-Arts*, May-June 1990, pp. 241-8; Weinglass

227 x 250 (194 x 235)

This picture, which did not fall into any of the conventional categories, made Fuseli famous after it was exhibited. It was clearly concerned with sexual assault and aroused great interest; Smith is said to have given Fuseli £20 in order to publish it and to have made £500 from the print. The picture may, as Powell suggests, reflect Fuseli's unfulfilled passion, but Moffitt has shown that it reveals Fuseli's knowledge of a work on witchcraft first published in 1487. Fuseli's friend Erasmus Darwin was inspired by the picture to write the verses which were engraved below Burke's print:

> *—- on his Night Mare, thro the evening fog,*
> *Flits the squab-fiend o'er fen, and lake, and bog;*
> *Seeks some love-wilder'd maid, by sleep opprest,*
> *Alights, and grinning, sits upon her breast.*

These were the opening lines to a longer, and very lurid, description of the picture in *The Loves of the Plants* which was eventually published in Darwin's *Botanic Garden* in 1789 (quoted by Powell pp. 58-60).

Thomas Burke (1749-1815) trained as a mezzotint engraver; he worked for the publisher and engraver W.W.Ryland in the 1770s, for whom he began to work in stipple in 1775, engraving many prints after Kauffman. In the early 1780s he began to work for other publishers, engraving a variety of subject pictures, including some of the paintings Kauffman sent back from Rome (No. 20).

7. HENRY AND EMMA

Colour-printed stipple by Robert Marcuard, 1783, after a drawing by Thomas Stothard illustrating Matthew Prior's *Henry and Emma*

(oval 195 x 155)

Matthew Prior (1664-1721) based his poem on the ballad of *The Nut-Brown Maid,* in which to test the Maid's devotion the well-born lover tells her that he is a banished man and that she will have to share his hardships. Henry is shown wooing Emma in the guise of a fortune teller; the same scene was treated by Kauffman (No. 21).

Robert Marcuard (1759-92) was a pupil of Bartolozzi, with whom he worked closely up to his early death; his prints were almost exclusively subject stipples.

8. THE PARTING OF HOTSPUR AND LADY PERCY

Colour-printed stipple by an anonymous engraver, one of a pair published by William Dickinson, 26 June 1784, after a drawing by Henry Bunbury, illustrating a ballad in Thomas Percy's *Reliques of Ancient Poetry,* 1765.

(subject 535 x 450)

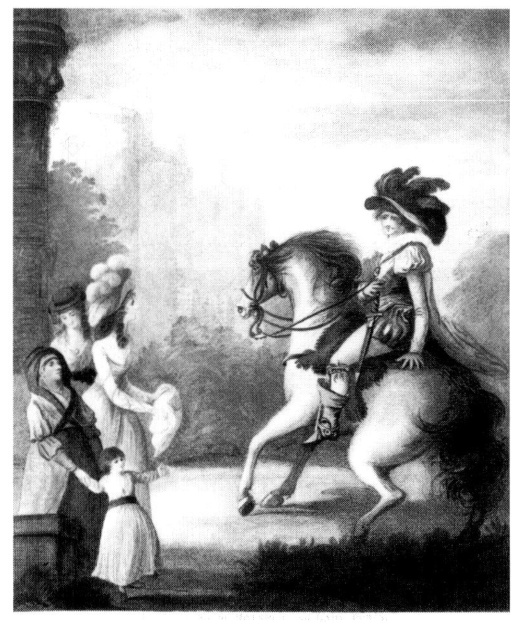

The Parting of Hotspur and Lady Percy

This print is typical of the many stipples produced after drawings by Henry Bunbury (Fig. 4). He was the younger son of a Norfolk landowner, and moved in the most fashionable circles. He was lauded by Horace Walpole, who called him 'the second Hogarth'; and albums of his prints were to be found in the libraries of many country houses. This print is dedicated to Lady Williams-Wynn, wife of a very powerful Welsh landowner; Bunbury was one of those who took part in amateur theatricals, which were very fashionable, often performing at Wynnstay, the Wynn family house, and many of his young ladies look as if they are still wearing their acting clothes.

William Dickinson (1746-1823) was a mezzotint engraver who largely abandoned engraving in favour of print publishing during the 1780s; he had a shop in Bond Street and a successful business but went bankrupt after the print trade contracted in the mid-1790s.

9. LORD THOMAS AND FAIR ANNETT
Stipple by Francesco Bartolozzi, published by William Dickinson, 1784, after a drawing by Henry Bunbury illustrating one of the ballads in Thomas Percy's *Reliques of Ancient Poetry,* 1765.
505 x 358 (circle 300 diam.)

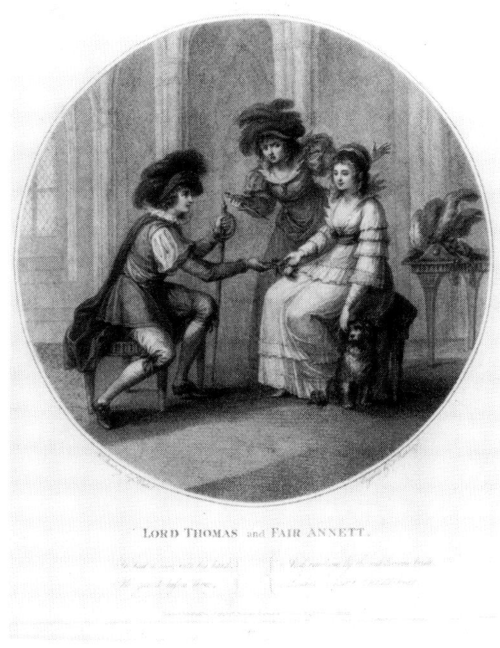

Lord Thomas and Fair Annett

Lord Thomas and Annett had a lovers' quarrel and he offered marriage to the wealthy Nut-Brown Maid. In the church he presented Annett with a rose, whereupon the Maid killed her with 'a bodkin from her headgear'. Lord Thomas stabbed first the Maid and then himself.

Francesco Bartolozzi (1725-1815), who signed this print, came to England as a line engraver in the 1760s and was a founder member of the Royal Academy on its inception in 1768. For twenty years, between about 1780 and 1800, he was the most celebrated stipple engraver, running a large studio with assistants and pupils. He often prettified drawings sent to him - unnecessary here - and improved their draughtsmanship, which was often very necessary in Bunbury's case.

10. A TALE OF LOVE
Stipple by J.K.Sherwin, published by James Bretherton, 1786, after a drawing by Henry Bunbury, with verses by William Shenstone.
462 x 375 (415 x 350)

Although this print may not strictly be a literary illustration it shows the way in which well-born ladies were at the fore both as readers and as purchasers of prints. It shows a group of elegant women reading poetry:

Come listen to my mournful tale,
Ye tender hearts and lovers dear;
Nor will you scorn to heave a sigh,
Nor need you blush to shed a tear.

Like many of Bunbury's drawings this belonged to a member of the aristocracy, in this case the Countess of Sutherland, to whom the publisher has dedicated the print.

John Keyse Sherwin (1751-90) was the son of a Sussex labourer; his great artistic gifts were detected while he was a child and he was trained as an engraver in line and stipple under Bartolozzi. Sherwin had an attractive personality and he was taken up by fashionable hostesses, who vied, for example, to be represented as attendants in a picture which he painted and engraved of *The Finding of Moses* with the Princess Royal as Pharaoh's daughter. Such activities took him away from the work to which he was best fitted; he got into financial difficulties and died young.

11. BIRTHA
12. ELEANOR OF BRETAGNE
Pair of stipple engravings by Caroline Watson, published by R.Cribb, 18 January 1785, after miniatures by Samuel Shelley, illustrating Hannah More's *St. Eldred of the Tower* and William Shenstone's *Elegy* XXIV.
c.200 x 155 (ovals c. 85 x 105)

Most miniature painters were solely concerned with portraiture but Samuel Shelley (1750-1808) also painted a considerable number of miniatures of historical and literary figures, many of which were engraved in stipple, whose scale was ideally suited to reproducing them. He was a founder member of the Old Watercolour Society established in 1804.

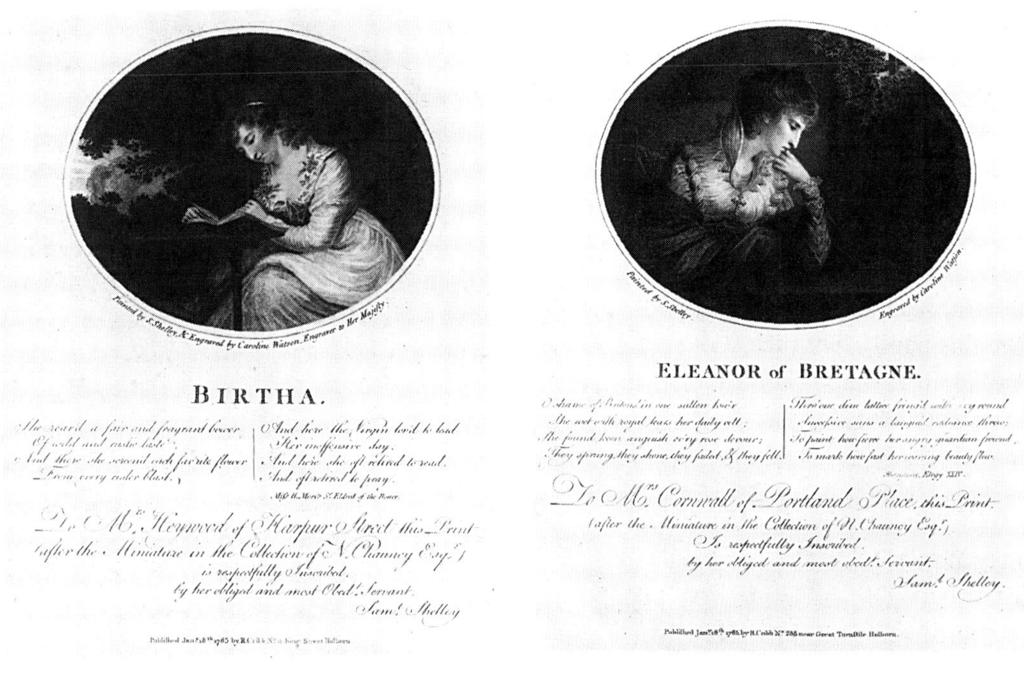

Birtha *Eleanor of Bretagne*

William Shenstone (1714-63), a pastoral poet, is remembered now primarily for his literary friendships and his efforts as a gardener at his small estate, the Leasowes, in Warwickshire. Hannah More (1745-1823) made a literary name for herself as a very young woman and was a protegée of the actor David Garrick and his wife; however by the time this print was published she was devoting her energies to good works and felt that many of her youthful activities had been unforgiveably frivolous.

Caroline Watson (1760-1814) was the daughter of the mezzotint engraver James Watson, who probably trained her although he did not work in the stipple technique, which was hardly used until 1775. She was encouraged by Queen Charlotte and was appointed Engraver to the Queen in 1785. She did some exquisite work, much of it on a small scale, but also engraved some larger prints (see No. 56) and was employed, apparently on Reynolds's request, to engrave his *Death of Cardinal Beaufort,* painted for Boydell's *Shakespeare.*

13. A SNAKE IN THE GRASS

Stipple engraved and published by J.R.Smith, 1787, after the painting by Sir Joshua Reynolds exhibited at the Royal Academy in 1784 and now in the Tate Gallery, published with verses by R.B.Cooper.

Lit: Frankau 326; E.Hamilton, *The Engraved Works of . . .Reynolds,* 1884, p.158.

(subject 255 x 205)

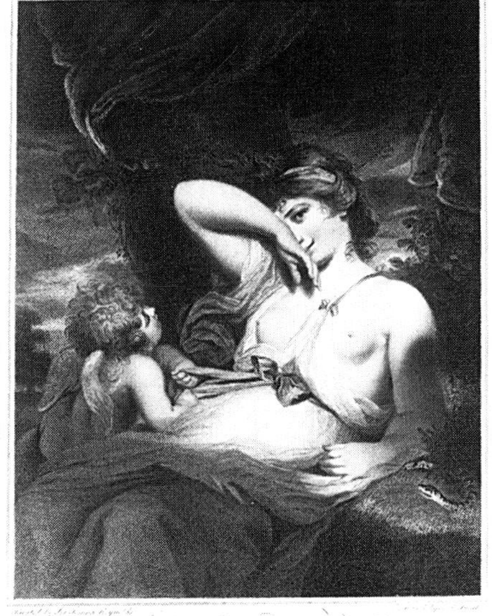

A Snake in the Grass

This picture was one of Reynolds's best known fancy pictures, of which he made several repetitions; it was later engraved on a larger scale in mezzotint by William Ward, Smith's pupil. The picture was exhibited as 'A Nymph and Cupid'. The verses engraved below the print, which begin

> *Fann'd by the summer's gentlest wind*
> *Within the shade a Nymph reclin'd*

may have been inspired by the picture. They are signed 'R.B.Cooper', who may be Robert Bransby Cooper, a lawyer born in 1762. It is possible that he may have contributed the verses to a magazine after seeing the picture at the Royal Academy.

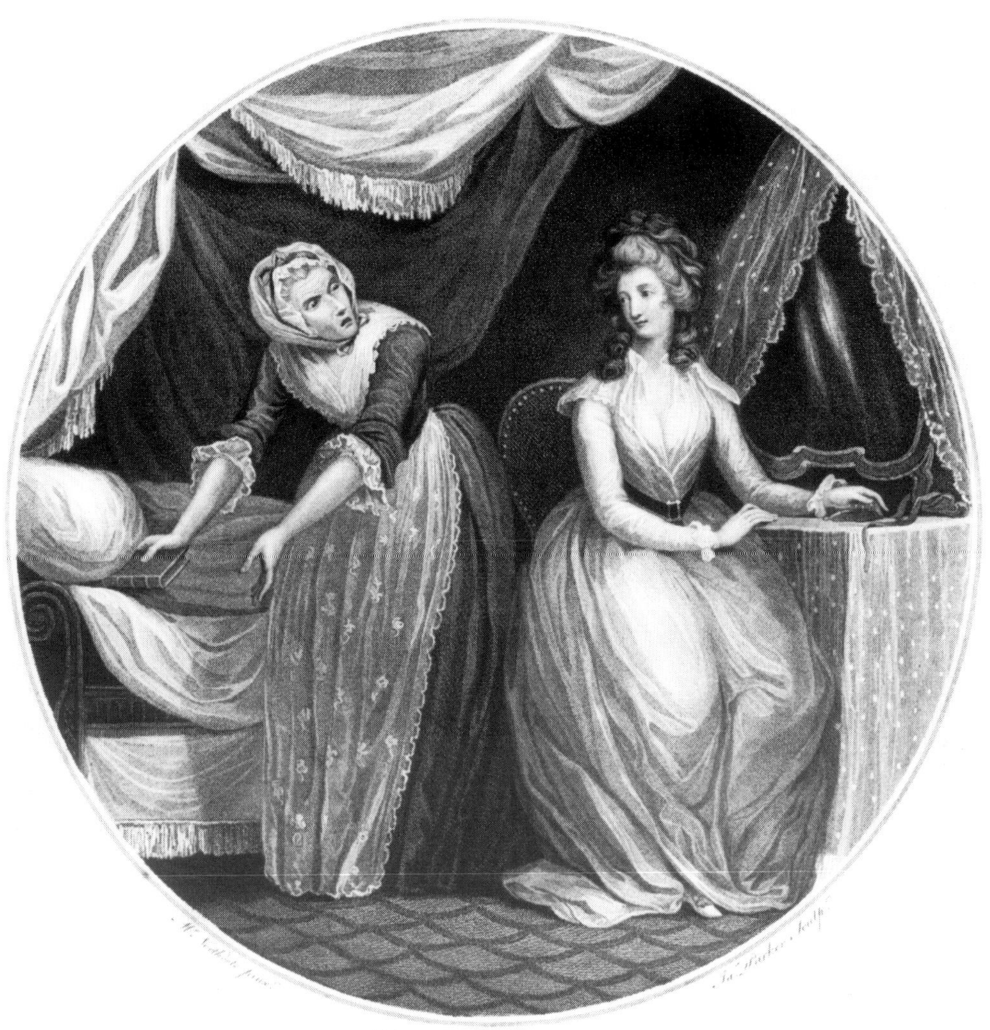

The Novel

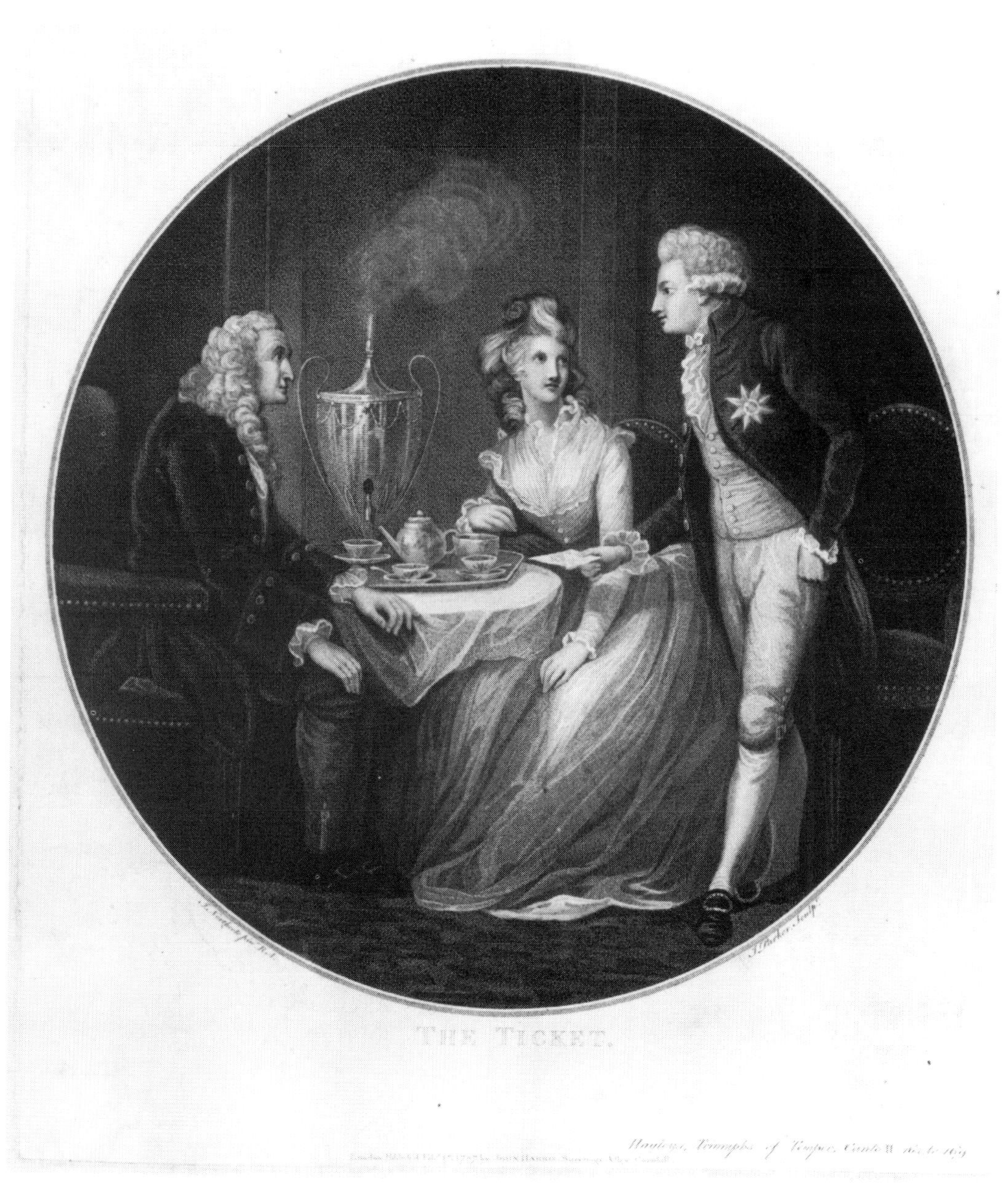

The Ticket

14. THE NOVEL
15. THE TICKET

Pair of stipples by James Parker, published by James Harris, 1787, after paintings by James Northcote illustrating William Hayley's *The Triumphs of Temper,* 1781.

c. 370 x 315 (circles 300 diam.)

This long poem - it is over three thousand lines - was the best known work by Hayley, friend and patron of many writers and artists, most notably George Romney and William Blake - who was described before his death as 'the work-basket poet of that day. His verses were upon every Girl's Sopha'. The poem was, in his own words 'intended to promote the cultivation of good humour', and it used the story of the heroine, Serena, to point lessons for young ladies. Perhaps because it was so well known the publisher felt it unnecessary to engrave the relevant verses at the foot of the prints. *The Novel* shows Serena's prim aunt finding her in possession of a novel:

Beneath the pillow, not completely hid,
The novel lay- She saw - She seiz'd - She chid;
With rage and glee her glaring eye-balls flash,
Ah wicked age ! She cries, ah filthy trash !

Whereupon she rushes off to read the book herself.

The Ticket shows Serena receiving an engraved invitation - clearly visible as a masked cupid - from the elegant Lord Filigree

The blushing maid, with eyes of quick desire
View'd it, and felt her little soul on fire;
For of all scenes she had not yet survey'd
Her heart most panted for a masquerade !

It is hard at times to know when Hayley is being flippant and when he is being serious. His contemporaries found the same difficulty and did not know what to make of his *Essay on Old Maids,* 1785; this lost him some of his most loyal readers, since many old maids thought that he was poking fun at them rather than extolling their virtues.

The first illustrated edition of the poem appears to be that of 1787, with plates after Stothard; there was another edition in 1803 with plates engraved by Blake after designs by Maria Flaxman.

James Parker (1750-1805) was a stipple engraver who executed other prints of literary paintings for Harris, including two circles after James Northcote illustrating Sterne (Painted Word Nos 50, 69) and two after Stothard illustrating Dr Johnson (Painted Word Nos 93-94). For a short time he and William Blake were in partnership as printsellers.

16. THE DEATH OF CORA
Colour-printed stipple by Bartolozzi, published as one of a pair by Mary Ryland, 1 May 1788, after a drawing by Henry Ramberg illustrating Helen Maria Williams's poem *Peru,* 1784.
262 x 187 (oval 197 x 160)

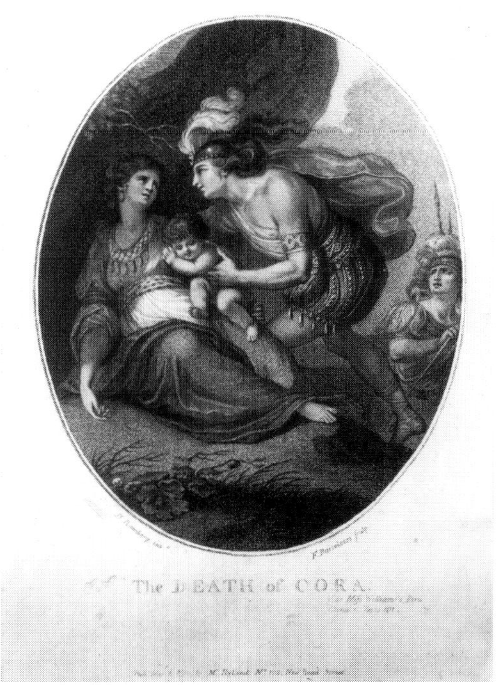

The Death of Cora

Helen Maria Williams (1762-1827), a young poet who was admired by the aged Dr Johnson, wrote her poem to give not a history of Peru but

> *a simple detail of a few incidents in this affecting and romantic History;*
> *where the unparalleled sufferings of an innocent and amiable People afford*
> *the finest subjects for true pathos...*

There is an implication in such an explanation that the feelings of the author are really more interesting than the sufferings described. The charge of insincerity was inevitably levelled at much sentimental posturing, though this particular poet was sincere enough in her sympathy for the oppressed. She moved to France in 1788 and was one of the few Britons to remain loyal to the ideals of the French Revolution, in which she was imprisoned and narrowly escaped with her life.

This print shows a defeated Inca finding his wife dying of exhaustion and exposure after searching for him. With her last breath she exclaims

> *My suff'ring heart is cold and mists arise*
> *That shroud thy image from my closing eye -*
> *Save my soft child - our tender infant save -*
> *And shed a tear upon thy CORA's grave.*

The print was based on a drawing by a young artist from Hanover Johann Heinrich Ramberg (1763-1840), who studied in England in the 1780s. He sold a number of drawings of literary subjects to Mary Ryland, widow of the engraver W.W.Ryland (see No. 38) and other publishers (see Nos 41-42).

17. PEGGY AND PATIE

Stipple designed and engraved by C.G.Playter, published by Edward Hedges, 29 September 1786, illustrating Allan Ramsay's *Gentle Shepherd,* 1725
278 x 202 (oval 185 x 150)

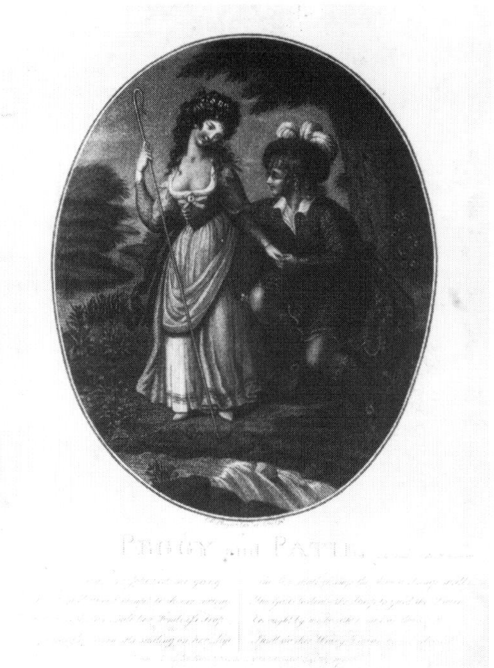

Peggy and Patie

Charles Gauthier Playter (active by 1778-d.1809) was a stipple engraver who engraved a number of literary prints, including two of four Shakespearian scenes after Samuel Shelley published by R.Cribb in 1786-7; he was also employed on Boydell's *Shakespeare.* This print precedes the twelve aquatint plates which the Scottish artist David Allan (1744-96) designed and engraved for an edition of this engaging pastoral drama by Allan Ramsay (1686-1758), the Edinburgh bookseller who was father of the portrait painter.

This print illustrates the passage

Peggy *I darna stay, ye Joker let me gang*
Or swear ye'll never tempt to do me wrang.
Patie *Sooner a Mother shall her Fondness drap,*
And wrang the Bairn sits smiling on her Lap.
The Sun shall change, the Moon to change shall cease,
The Gaits to dim - the Sheep to yield the Fleece
Ere ought by me-be either said or doon,
Shall do thee Wrang I swear by all aboon.

18. LOUISA

Stipple by Thomas Gaugain, published by J.R.Smith as one of a pair, 10 April 1789, after a painting by George Morland illustrating Jane Bowdler's Louisa, from *Poems and Essays,* 1786.
(oval 395 x 330)

The works of the invalid Jane Bowdler enjoyed considerable popularity after her death in 1784, and had gone into sixteen editions by 1830, being sold in aid of a Bath hospital. The poet, a sister of the editor whose name has entered the language on account of the expurgations he carried out on Shakespeare's texts, was a member of the literary group assembled by Lady Miller at Batheaston during the 1770s; their poetical effusions appeared in four volumes of *Poetical Amusements.*

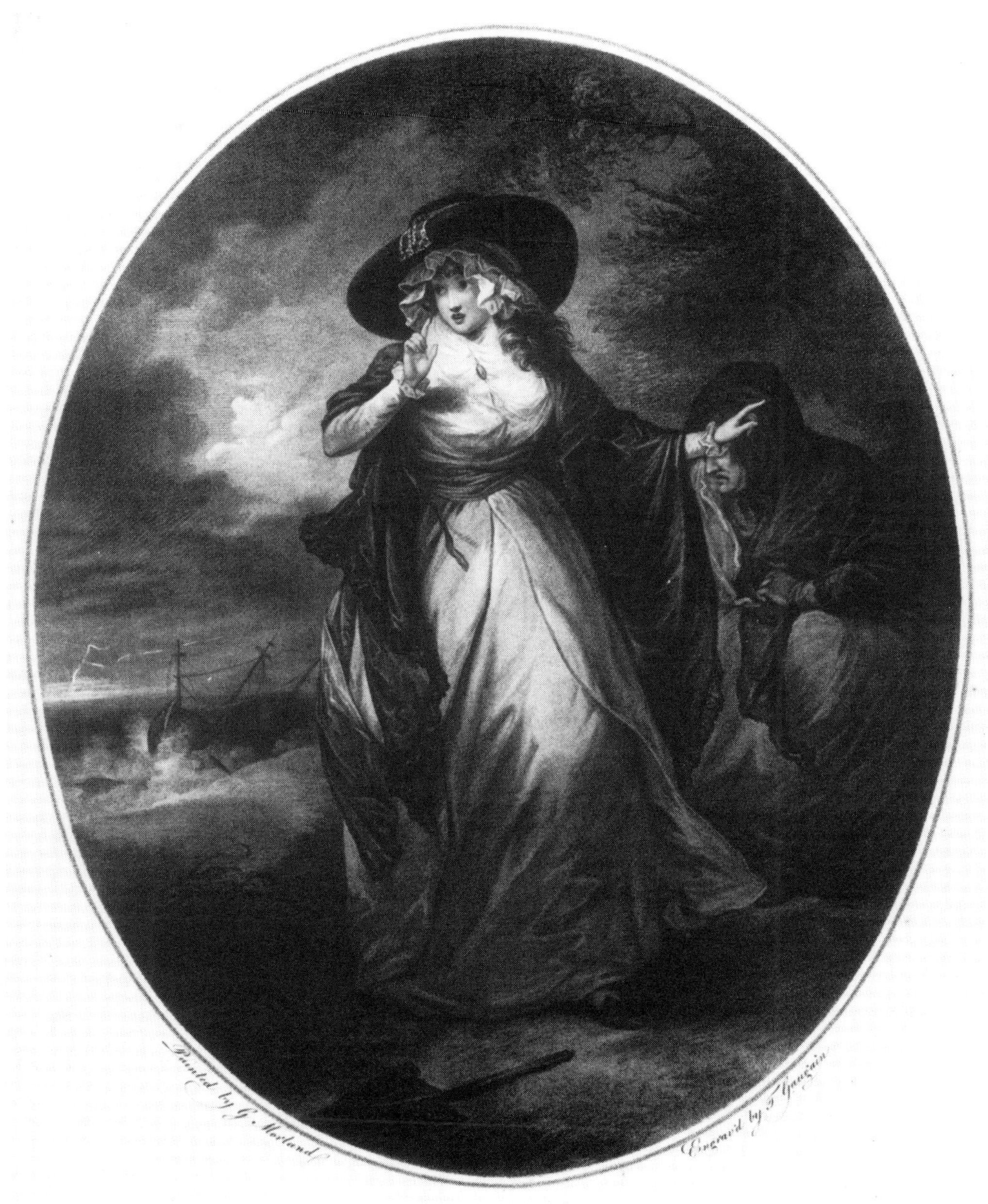
Painted by G. Morland
Engrav'd by T. Gaugain
LOUISA
O My life! my joy! my only love!
A voice at distance cries
That voice her inmost soul could move
She starts with wild surprise.

Louisa

Bowdler's work had a strong moral tone: Louisa is shown at a critical moment when the ship carrying her father and sweetheart is suddenly shipwrecked before her eyes. They are in fact saved and Louisa describes a glowing picture of wholesome poverty with her beloved, unthreatened by the temptations which wealth brings.

George Morland (1763-1804) was best known for his rustic genre pictures of the late 1780s and 1790s which were engraved in mezzotint, many of them engraved and published by J.R.Smith; however he also painted a number of subject pictures which were engraved in stipple.

Thomas Gaugain (1756-c.1810) was a painter who became a stipple engraver and engraved and published many successful subject prints; like many of his colleagues he had to give up printselling in the difficult economic climate of the 1790s.

19. A COUNTRY CHURCHYARD

Aquatint by Maria Catherina Prestel, published by Robert Pollard, 1790, after the painting by Thomas Gainsborough exhibited at the Royal Academy in 1780.
Lit: John Hayes, *Gainsborough as a Printmaker,* London, 1972, ill. p. 70.
(Impression cut down from subject size 465 x 635)

This print is suggestive of the literary climate which saw allusions to literature as a way of selling prints. Gainsborough was not interested in painting literary illustrations, and this picture was not associated with Thomas Gray's *Elegy in a Country Churchyard* when it was exhibited, but there are grounds for believing that the painter had had the poem in mind. Robert Pollard, who issued this print two years after Gainsborough's death, thought the link strong enough to print the first sixteen lines of the poem beneath the image.

Maria Catherina Prestel (1747-94) was wife of the Nuremberg painter and engraver Johann Gottleib Prestel, who used aquatint to reproduce old master drawings. She engraved some aquatints in Germany; most of her prints were engraved after she left her husband and moved in 1786 to London where she engraved a number of large landscape aquatints for publishers. At that time she and Caroline Watson were the only women working as independent engravers, though others worked for family teams.

Robert Pollard (1755-1838) was an engraver (see No. 41) who published many aquatints and subject plates; his business was over-extended when the print trade contracted in the 1790s, but he kept his stock of copper plates hoping that demand for them would revive; taste had moved on and he was eventually forced to sell them for low prices. His son Robert became a celebrated painter of sporting and coaching scenes, which, engraved in aquatint and brilliantly hand-coloured, represented a new genre of print which was in great demand.

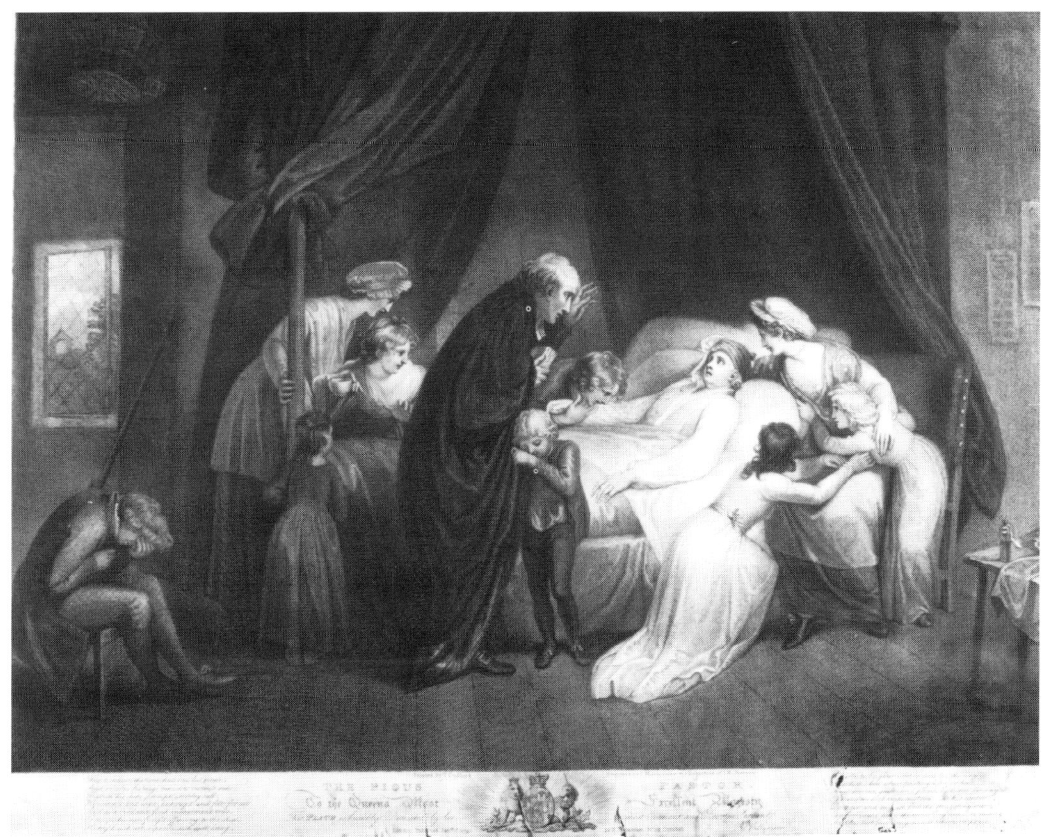

The Pious Pastor

20. THE PIOUS PASTOR
Stipple engraved by S.Miller 'under the Inspection of I.K.Sherwin', published by R.Wilkinson, I January 1791, after a painting by Stothard illustrating Oliver Goldsmith's *Deserted Village.*
(subject 450 x 560)

No selection of prints of the period would be representative without a death scene; various heroic deaths, notably that of General Wolfe at Quebec, engraved by William Woollett after the picture by Benjamin West, were among the best-selling prints of the century. Here Stothard shows the idealised view of the village pastor presented by Goldsmith; such pictures were to become reassuring symbols in an unequal society whose assumptions were so rudely challenged by the French Revolution, an event which made many thoughtful people realise how privileged their secure lives were.

The print is dedicated to Queen Charlotte who was becoming a keen print collector at the time that it was published.

21. HENRY AND EMMA

Stipple engraved by Thomas Burke, one of a pair published by J & J.Boydell, 2 Jan 1792, after a painting by Angelica Kauffman illustrating Matthew Prior's *Henry and Emma.*
(circle 335 diam.)

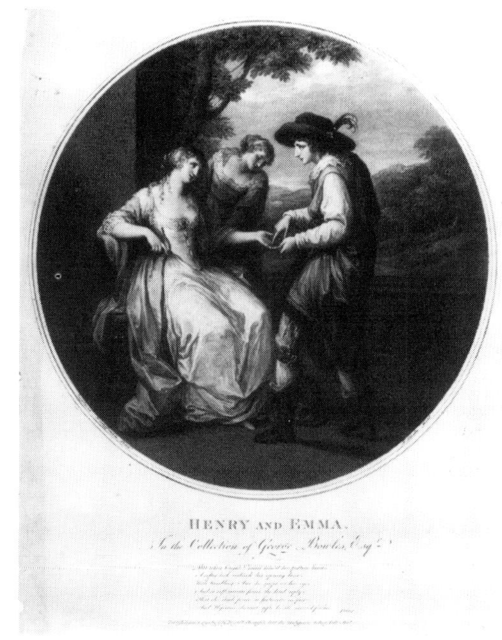

Henry and Emma

As in the print after Stothard (No.7) Henry is shown wooing Emma in the guise of a fortune teller. This is one of a number of pictures of English literature painted by Kauffman who was in England from 1766 to 1781; she painted a large number of pictures illustrating Greek and Roman classics, many of which were engraved first in mezzotint and then after 1775 in stipple, but during the 1780s taste for illustrations of the ancient classics gave way to the demand for prints of modern literature. George Bowles, to whom this print is dedicated, was one of the most enthusiastic collectors of her work and she continued to paint pictures for him - as she did for London printsellers - after she left England for Italy. The print was paired with *Angelica and Sacriponte,* from Aristo; they were sold for 7/6d each uncoloured.

22. ETHELINDA RESTORED TO HER FATHER

Colour-printed stipple by R.M.Meadows, published by J.R.Smith, 1793, after a painting by Thomas Stothard illustrating Sophia Lee's *The Hermit's Tale,* 1787.
(subject cut to 255 x 310)

Sophia Lee (1750-1824) who ran a school with her sister in Bath, followed up her successful novel *The Recess* (see Nos. 53-54) with a long poem *The Hermit's Tale,* 'recorded by his own hand and found in his cell.' The Hermit, Edmund, had been a simple northern shepherd at the time of the Crusades, but becomes a renowned warrior against the marauding Scots. He rescues the high-born Ethelinda and is shown here returning her to her father. The young couple have fallen in love, but her father has plans for her to marry an older man, Baron Albert. The two suitors fight, and as he is dying Albert realises that Edmund is his son. Meanwhile the despairing Ethelinda has taken poison. In his sorrow Edmund becomes a hermit.

Robert Mitchell Meadows (1763-c.1812) worked exclusively in stipple; at the end of the 1790s he was the principal engraver employed by Richard Westall, who published a number of stipples of his genre pictures.

23. ALCANZOR AND ZAIDA
Colour-printed stipple by Francesco Bartolozzi after his own drawing, published by H.Freeman, 7 February 1796, illustrating the poem in Percy's *Reliques,* 1765.
(circle 310 diam.)

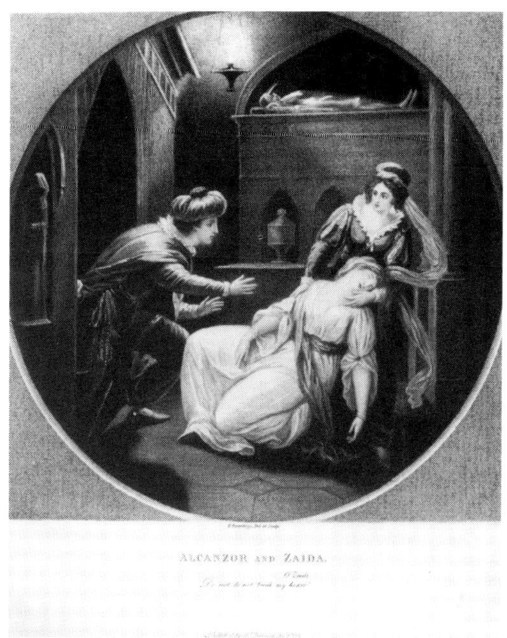

Alcanzor and Zaida

This print illustrates an Eastern tale of thwarted love in which Zaida tells her beloved that she will die of a broken heart because her father is forcing her to marry another. The artist has sacrificed accuracy in showing the lovers together: in the poem they talk through a window.

Although he was best known as a reproductive engraver, first in line and then in stipple, Bartolozzi was also an able artist in his own right and had been a founder member of the Royal Academy. He designed a number of decorative prints.

24. ROSEBUD, OR THE JUDGMENT OF PARIS
Colour-printed stipple by William Nutter, published by E.M.Diemar as a pair with *The Sensitive Plant,* 1796, and reissued by Ackermann, 1801, after a watercolour by Richard Westall, illustrating Matthew Prior's poem *A Lover's Anger,* exhibited at the Royal Academy in 1791 and now in the Yale Center for British Art, New Haven.
(subject 342 x 390)

This print illustrates Prior's poem in which a lover chides his sweetheart for being two hours late for their meeting:

Lord bless me ! said she, let a body but speak;
Here's an ugly hard rose bud fallen into my neck,
It has hurt me and vext me to such a degree
See here, for you never believe me, pray see
On the left side my breast what a mark it has made
So saying her bosom she carelessly display'd
That seat of delight I with wonder survey'd
And forgot every word I design'd to have said.

Richard Westall (1765-1836) was important as one of those who created the 'exhibition watercolour', a finished production which when impressively framed could compete with

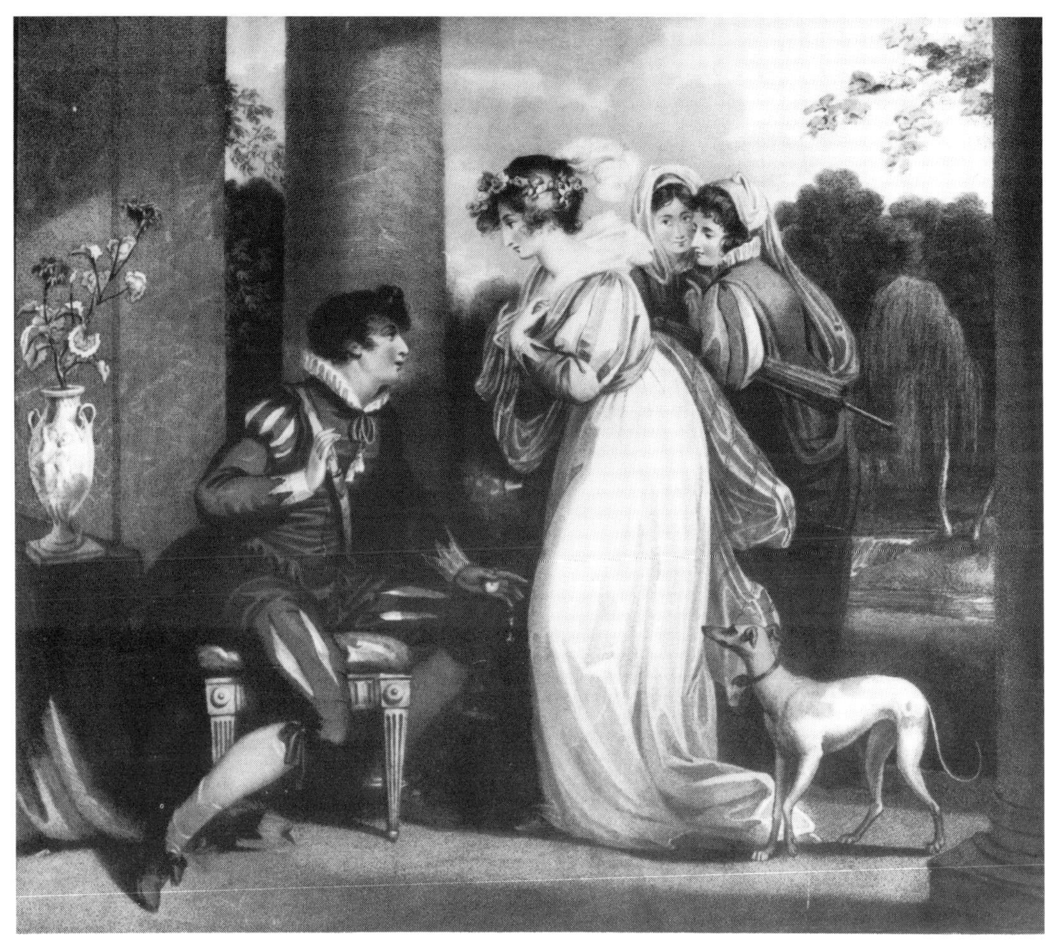

Rosebud, or the Judgment of Paris

oil paintings for collectors' attention. Many of his grand watercolours were engraved in aquatint, which could be hand coloured to imitate a watercolour, and such prints were among those which supplanted stipples after 1800. Westall himself published a number of very large and expensive aquatints which were virtually facsimiles of his watercolours, but his venture was not successful.

After the death of the original publisher, Mrs Diemar, this pair of plates was bought by Rudolph Ackermann, the publisher who most successfully gauged what would sell best in an England which was constantly at war with France until 1815. He was the publisher of some of the finest of colour plate books, illustrated with hand-coloured aquatints. He sold colour-printed impressions of this print and its companion for the large sum of a guinea and a half (£1-11-6); uncoloured proofs were £1-4-0 and ordinary impressions 15/-.

25-27. THE SORROWS OF LADY ALICE

Pair of stipple engravings, designed and engraved by Henry Richter, the first published by P. Contencin, 8 February 1796, the second by J. and H. Richter, 30 July 1797, together with a colour printed impression of the second framed in *verre eglomisée,* illustrating the ballad *The Sorrows of Lady Alice.*
Plates c. 370 x 265 (ovals c. 265 x 220)

This print illustrates a ballad which tells the tribulations of Alice, whose husband is murdered. In her demented grief she is confined by his brother and dreams that he is the murderer. *Verre eglomisée* is glass which has been painted black on the reverse; this was a popular way of framing prints at the time and made them look more impressive.

Henry Richter (1772-1857) was a painter in watercolour of German extraction who also engraved in stipple. He was a member of the Old Watercolour Society from 1813 and became known for his genre pictures.

28. THE WATER SPRITE

Stipple by Isaac Taylor Junior, published by Isaac Taylor, Colchester, 20 January 1798, after a drawing by Henry Bunbury illustrating the ballad in Matthew ('Monk') Lewis's novel *The Monk,* 1794.
(subject 280 x 400)

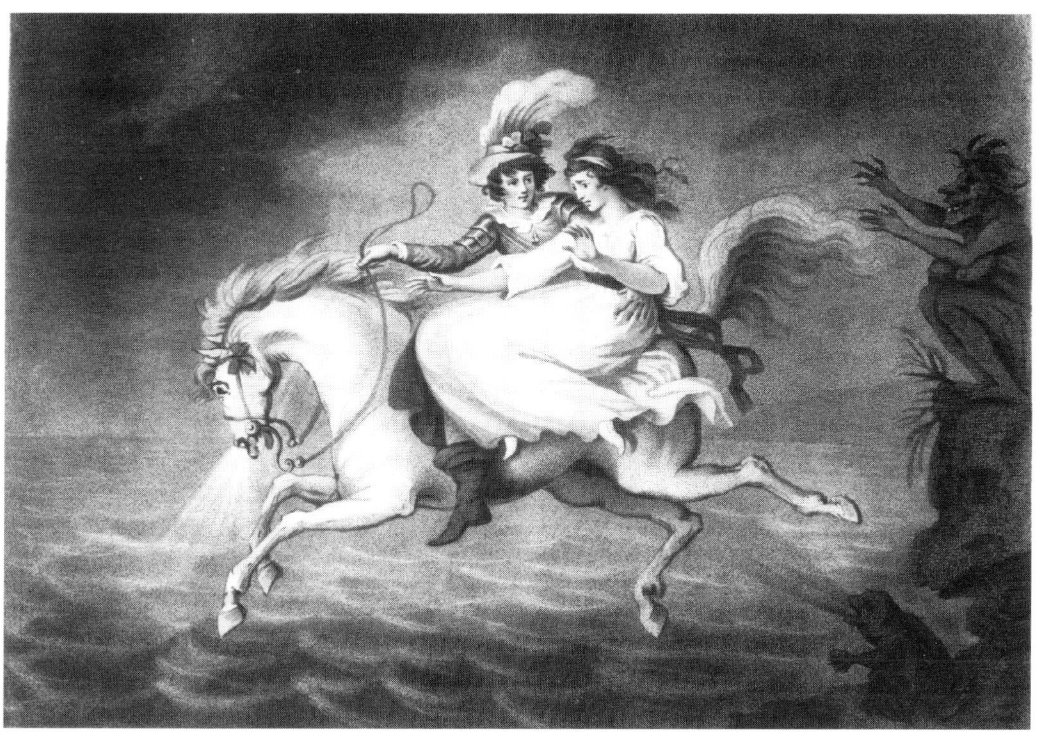

The Water Sprite

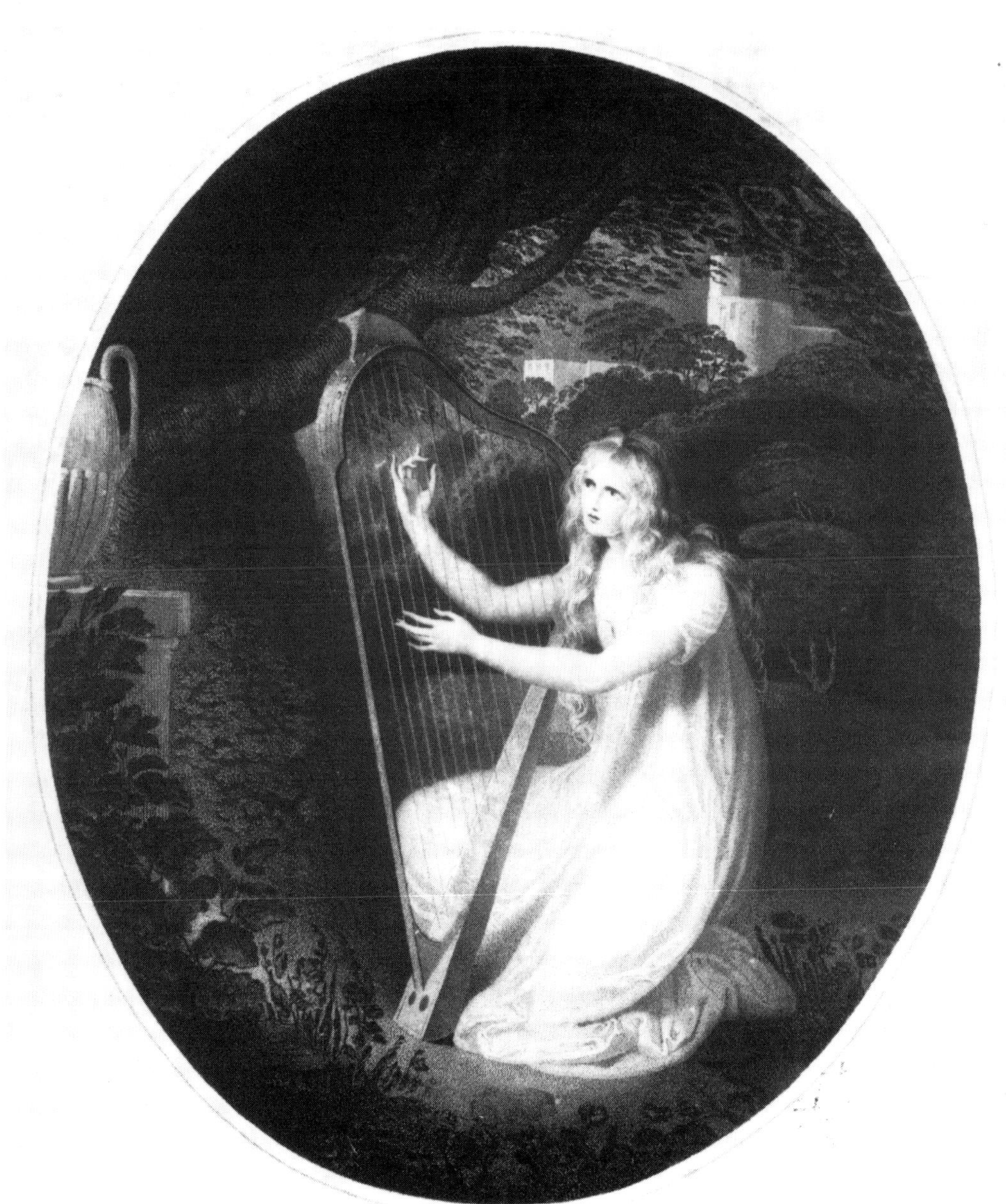

The Sorrows of Lady Alice

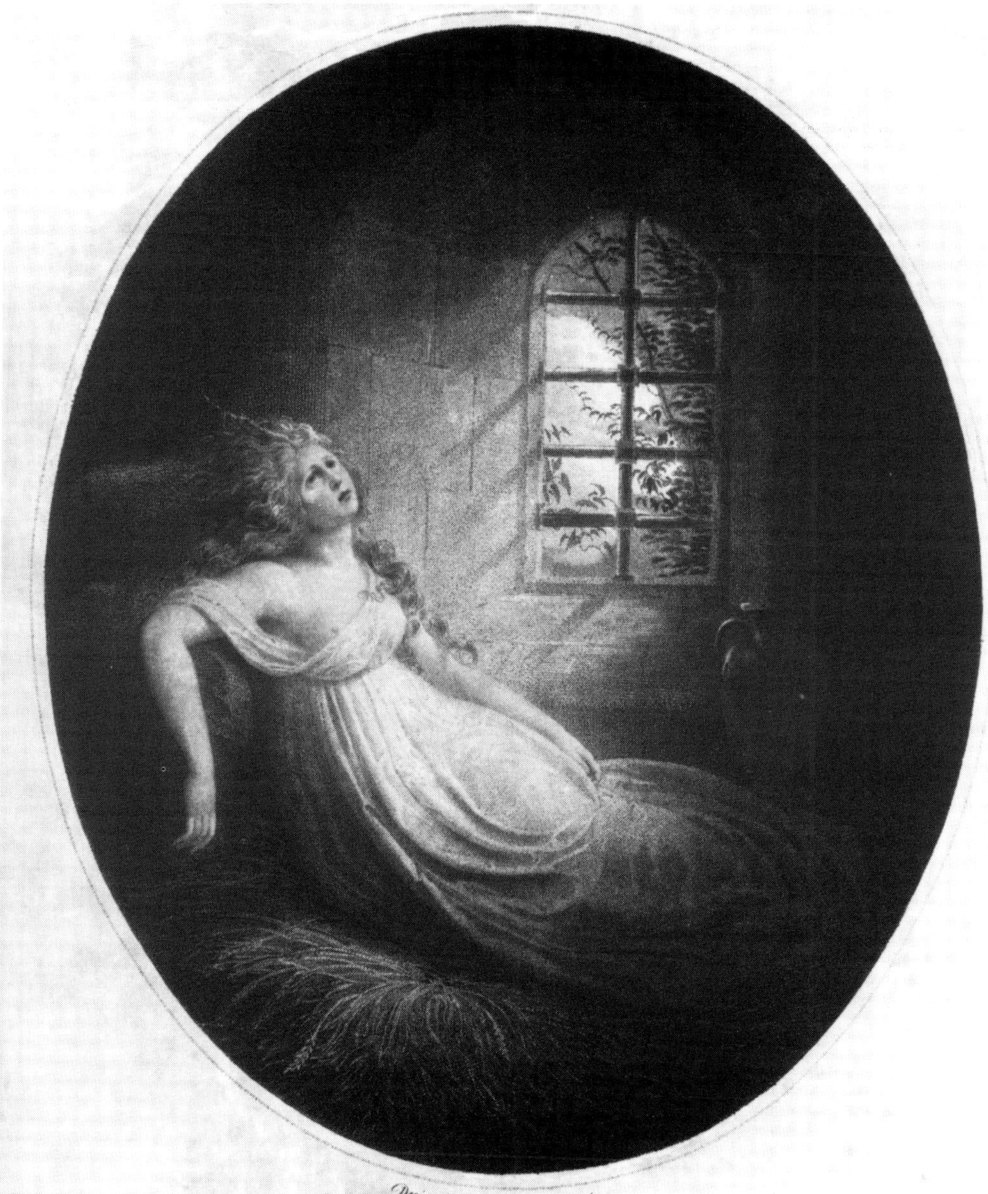

The Sorrows of Lady Alice

This print shows how weak Bunbury could be; he was incapable of conveying much of the feeling of Lewis's gothick romance, published when the author was 21. The verses read

Warned by this tale, ye damsels fair
To whom ye give your love beware;
Believe not every handsome Knight
And dance not with the Water Sprite.

The print is unusual in being one which was engraved outside London. Isaac Taylor (1750-1829), a London engraver who later became a non-conformist minister in East Anglia, moved in 1786 to Lavenham in Suffolk, where he continued to engrave for the London market; he was helped by his sons and by his daughters Jane and Ann, who became well known as writers.

29-33. PRINTS FROM MACKLIN'S 'POETS GALLERY'

29. PRINCE ARTHUR'S VISION

Stipple by P.W.Tomkins, published by Macklin in the first number of his 'British Poets', 4 April 1788, after a painting by Henry Fuseli illustrating Edmund Spencer's *Faerie Queen*, Book I, Canto IX.
Lit: V&C 1430; Weinglass.
(subject 451 x 353)

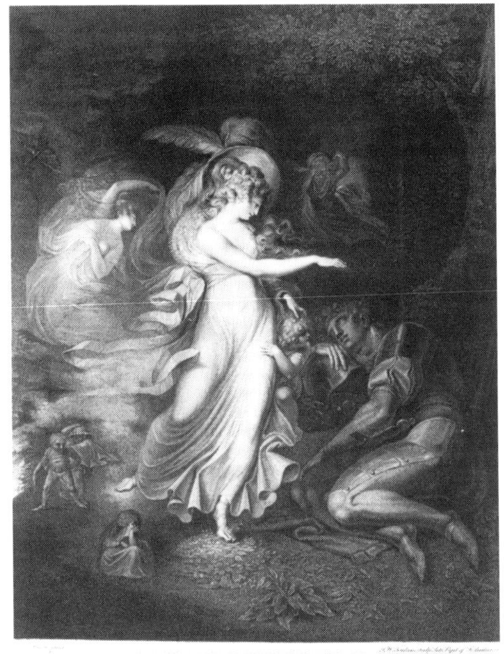

Prince Arthur's Vision

The sleeping Arthur has a dream of the Faerie Queen:

And slombring soft my hart did
steale away,
Me seemed, by my side a royall Mayd
Her daintie limbes full softly down
did lay:
So faire a creature yet saw never
sunny day.

He is inspired by his love for the Queen to join with her knights in their various adventures.

Peltro William Tomkins (1760-1840) was a pupil of Bartolozzi's, a fact that he long continued to put on his prints (e.g. No. 32). In 1793 he was appointed Engraver to Queen Charlotte.

30. THE ANTIENT ENGLISH WAKE

Stipple by J.Chapman, published by Macklin, 1794, after a painting by William Hamilton, illustrating Edward Jerningham's poem *The Ancient English Wake,* 1779.

432 x 510 (355 x 455)

The picture shows a daughter before her father, holding aloft her husband's heart in a casket, the object which has enabled her to survive years of foreign vicissitudes.

The numerous poems by Edward Jerningham (1727-1812) are little known today, but in his day were popular, not least because he was a well-born man with a wide aquaintance. He was associated with the Della Crusca group of poets, who produced a quantity of often very silly verse, which helped to discredit the affectations of sensibility. Among his later poems was one in praise of Boydell's 'Shakespeare Gallery'.

31. THE DESERTED VILLAGE

Stipple by Bartolozzi, published by Macklin, 1795, after a painting by Francis Wheatley illustrating Oliver Goldsmith's *Deserted Village,* 1770.

Lit: V&C 1440; Webster E 112, ill. p.178.

432 x 508

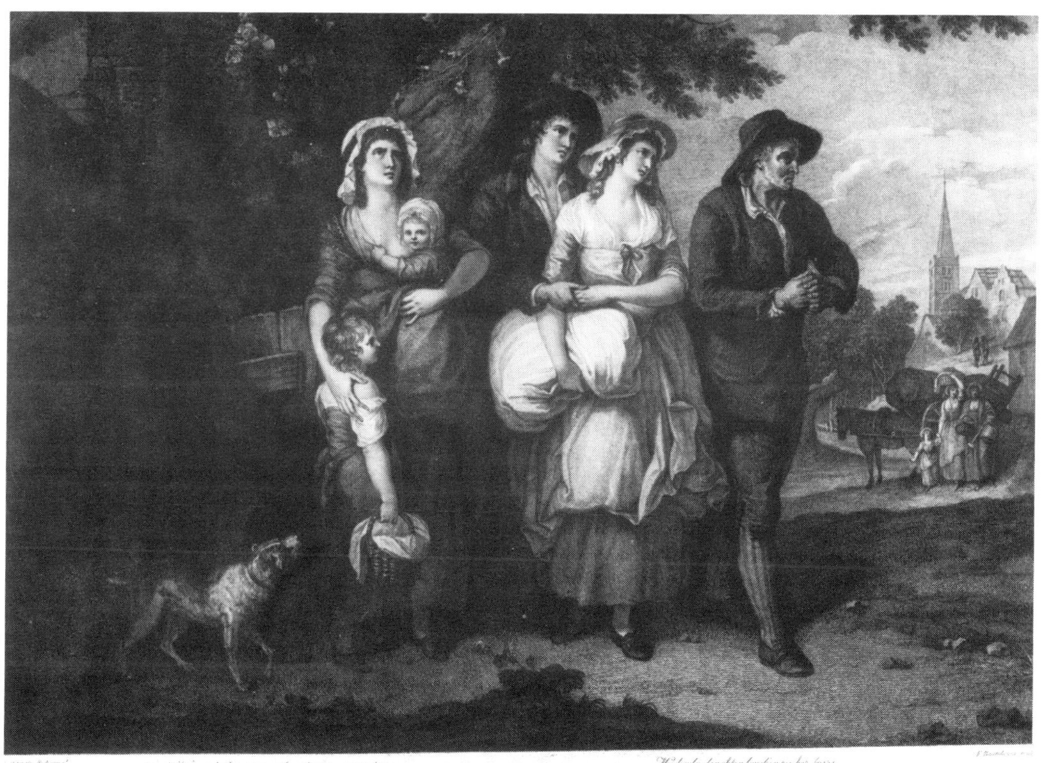

The Deserted Village

Goldsmith's poem attacked the apparently heartless way in which villagers were often moved to suit a landowner's convenience. This was often the sentimental view of the townsman: villagers were often happy to be moved to modern houses, as was done by Lord Harcourt at Nuneham Courtenay, the village which Goldsmith is thought to have had in mind.

Francis Wheatley (1747-1801) was one of painters most regularly employed by printsellers; he is best known for his idealised *Cries of London,* painted for the printseller Colnaghi and engraved 1793-6. His depictions of peasants are consistently sentimental, but the public was hardly likely to wish to see pictures that showed them other than clean and attractive.

32. AMYNTOR AND THEODORA
Colour-printed stipple by P.W.Tomkins, published by Macklin, 1796, after a painting by Stothard illustrating David Mallett's *Amyntor and Theodora, or the Hermit,* 1747.
Lit: Shelley Bennett, *Thomas Stothard,* Columbus, Miss., 1988, p. 22.
432 x 500 (355 x 455)

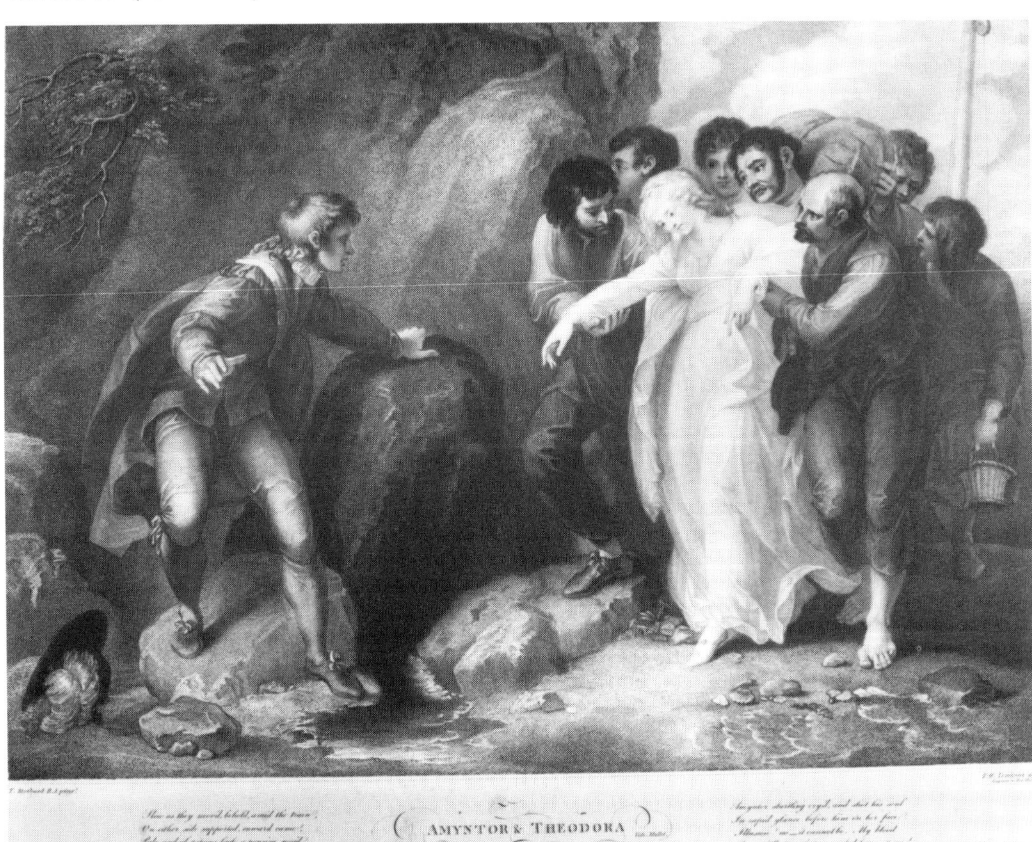

Amyntor and Theodora

This poem is set in the Hebrides, whose inhabitants are pictured as noble and uncorrupted. Amyntor, son of a mainland tyrant, is shipwrecked when escaping from his father's court with Theodora. He is saved and cared for by Aurelius, the hermit, who had been exiled by Amyntor's father and is, for a moment, tempted to kill the son. Theodora is thought to have been drowned; the picture shows Theodora, who is in fact Aurelius's daughter, being brought ashore, much to Amyntor's amazement.

Stothard was principally employed in making drawings and watercolours for book illustration, but he painted this picture in oil and it was exhibited in Macklin's Gallery from 1788.

33. GRAY'S ELEGY

Stipple by Bartolozzi, published by Macklin, 27 June 1799, after a painting by William Hamilton illustrating Thomas Gray's *Elegy in a Country Churchyard,* 1750.

Lit: V&C 1444

440 x 510 (355 x 455)

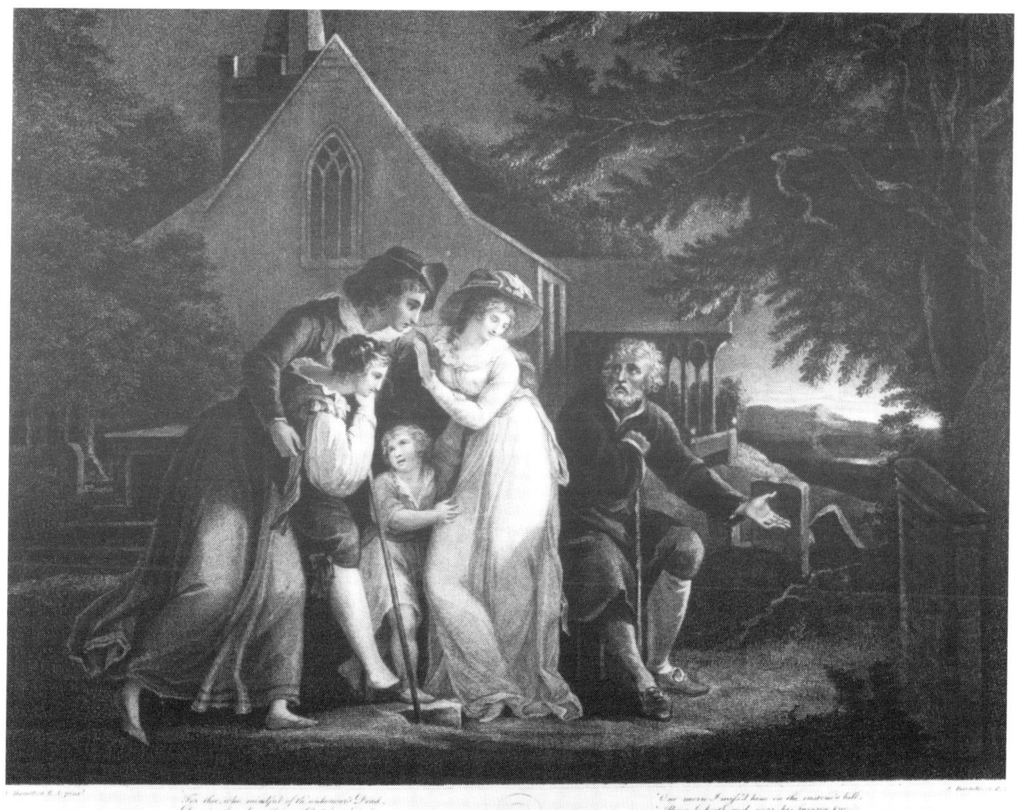

Gray's Elegy

This print, which carries four of the final six stanzas of the Elegy, shows Gray's 'hoary-headed Swain' pointing to the epitaph with which the poem concludes. This was perhaps the most obviously pictorial passage in the *Elegy,* and a picture by Gainsborough seems to refer to it (see No. 19). The same incident was depicted as the frontispiece to the poem in a remarkable publication, *Designs by Mr R.Bentley, from Six Poems by Mr T.Gray,* which appeared in 1753. (This volume, which was engineered by Horace Walpole, using the talents of his protegée Richard Bentley (1708-82), was one of the few outstanding works of book illustration in eighteenth century England and is the subject of a study by Loftus Jestin, *The Answer to the Lyre,* Philadelphia, 1990.)

34. THE FATHER'S ADMONITION
35. THE COUNTRY CLERGYMAN

Pair of stipples after drawings, the first by L.Schiavonetti after Wheatley, the second by R.Field after R.Westall with verses from Goldsmith's *Deserted Village,* published by Anthony Cardon, 1 March 1801.
Lit: Harry Piers, *Robert Field,* New York, 1927, No. CXLII
410 x 450 (330 x 405)

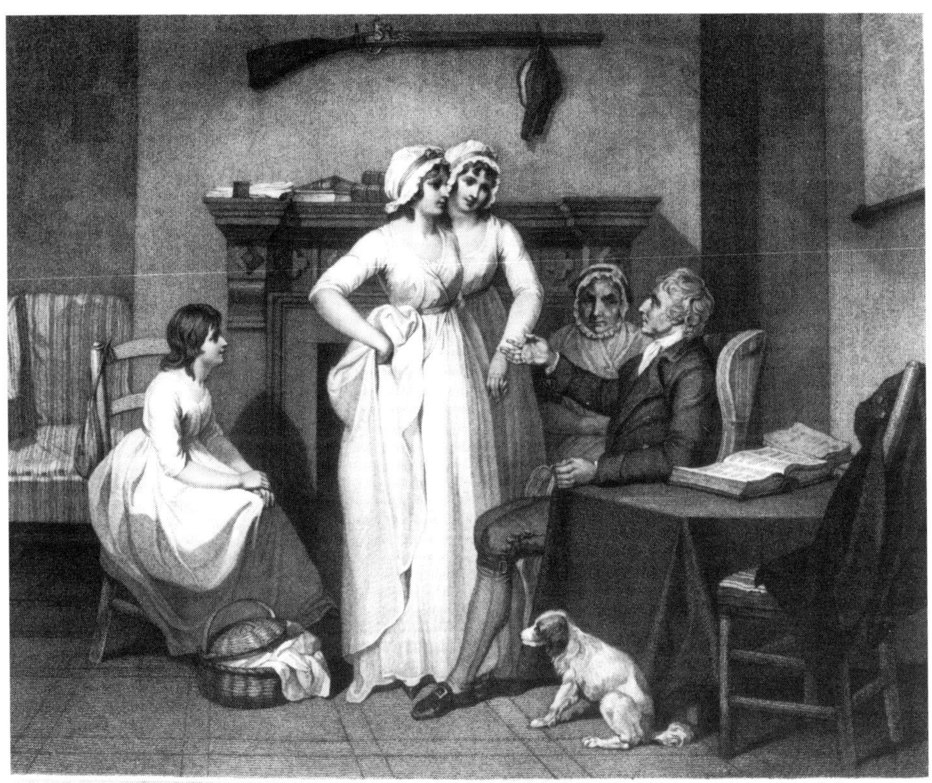

The Father's Admonition

These finely engraved plates project the comforting picture of a happy rural population, as seen also in Stothard's view of the parson (No. 20). In reality, of course, there were many country clergymen who were uncaring and perfunctory in their duties, as the poet William Crabbe (1754-1832) described in his poem about the rural poor, *The Village*, 1783, which was partly provoked by the persistence of Goldsmith's picture. Few artists chose Crabbe as a poet to paint, though Henry Singleton exhibited a picture of Crabbe's villain Peter Grimes two years after his appearance in *The Borough,* 1810.

Luigi Schiavonetti (1765-1810) was trained in Bassano before coming to England and initially worked with Bartolozzi; he often worked with Anthony Cardon (1772-1813), another stipple engraver, and they cooperated on some sucessful prints of incidents in the long war with France, producing the patriotic images which were in demand at the time. R.Field is presumably Robert Field (1769-1819), a portrait painter in oil and miniature who trained as an engraver. He went to the United States in 1794, but seems to have been in England c.1801-3; he was later in Boston, moving c.1808 to Nova Scotia and in 1816 to Jamaica where he died.

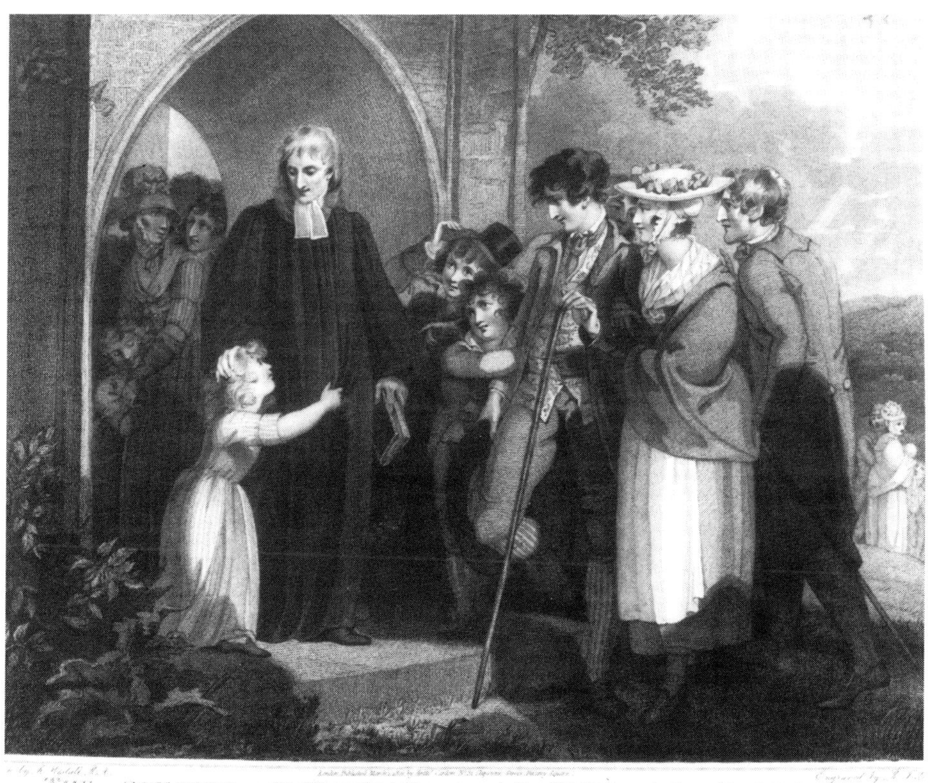

The Country Clergyman

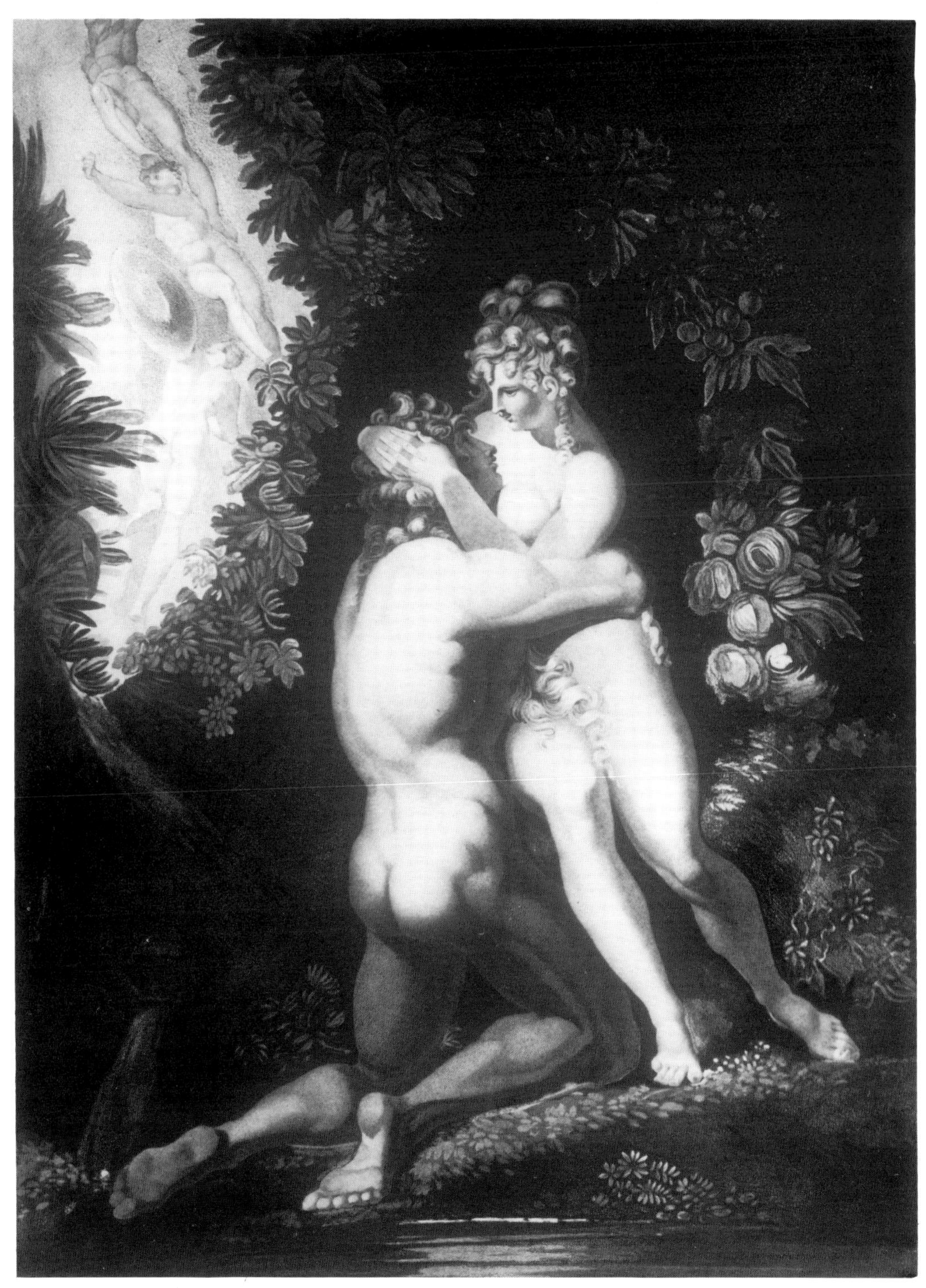

Adam resolved to share the fate of Eve

36. ADAM RESOLVED TO SHARE THE FATE OF EVE
Aquatint and stipple by Moses Haughton, published by Henry Fuseli after his painting illustrating John Milton's *Paradise Lost,* now in a Swiss private collection (Schiff 1214)
Lit; Pointon; Schiff; Weinglass
(subject 520 x 390)

Fuseli was an immensely well-read man; he was a particular admirer of Milton and painted some sixty pictures illustrating Miltonic episodes. He hoped to provide illustrations for William Cowper's projected edition, but this was no longer a viable proposition after the publication of a folio edition by Boydell with plates after designs by Richard Westall. Fuseli did not give up his plans for a series of prints after his Miltonic pictures, but decided to bring out singly issued prints himself rather than look for another publisher prepared to bring out an illustrated edition. In 1799 and 1800 he held two exhibitions of his Miltonic paintings, showing some forty-seven paintings, and planned a series of fifty prints from this 'Milton Gallery'. In the event fourteen prints by Moses Haughton (1772/4-1848), who lived in Fuseli's house and was his partner in the venture, appeared between 1803 and 1814. The picture was also engraved in 1802 for the edition of *Paradise Lost* published by F.J.Du Roveray.

37. THE WINTER DAY
Hand-coloured aquatint by Caroline Watson, proof before all letters, one of a set published by R.Ackermann, 1 March 1803, after drawings by Maria Cosway illustrating Mary Robinson's poem *The Winter Day.*
300 x 350 (subject 230 x 285)

Maria Cosway (1759-1838), wife of the miniature painter Richard Cosway, R.A., was a talented subject painter who made many designs for prints and also contributed to Boydell's *Shakespeare*. Mary Robinson (1758-1800), known as 'Perdita' from her short career on the stage, became well-known as the mistress of George, Prince of Wales, who discarded her. His treatment of her and a later illness which left her crippled aroused considerable sympathy for her. She made a name as a poet, associated with the Della Crusca group, publishing under such names as 'Laura Maria' and 'Oberon'; an elegant volume of her poems, printed by John Bell, was published by subscription in 1791. The Prince of Wales headed a list of some 550 subscribers, many of them drawn from the aristocracy; this was no dout a discreet way of giving her some financial help.

This print, the fifth in the set, illustrates the verses

Is it to haunt in warm attire
To laugh & feast & dance & sing,
To crowd around the blazing fire
And make the roof with revels ring
Ah! No!

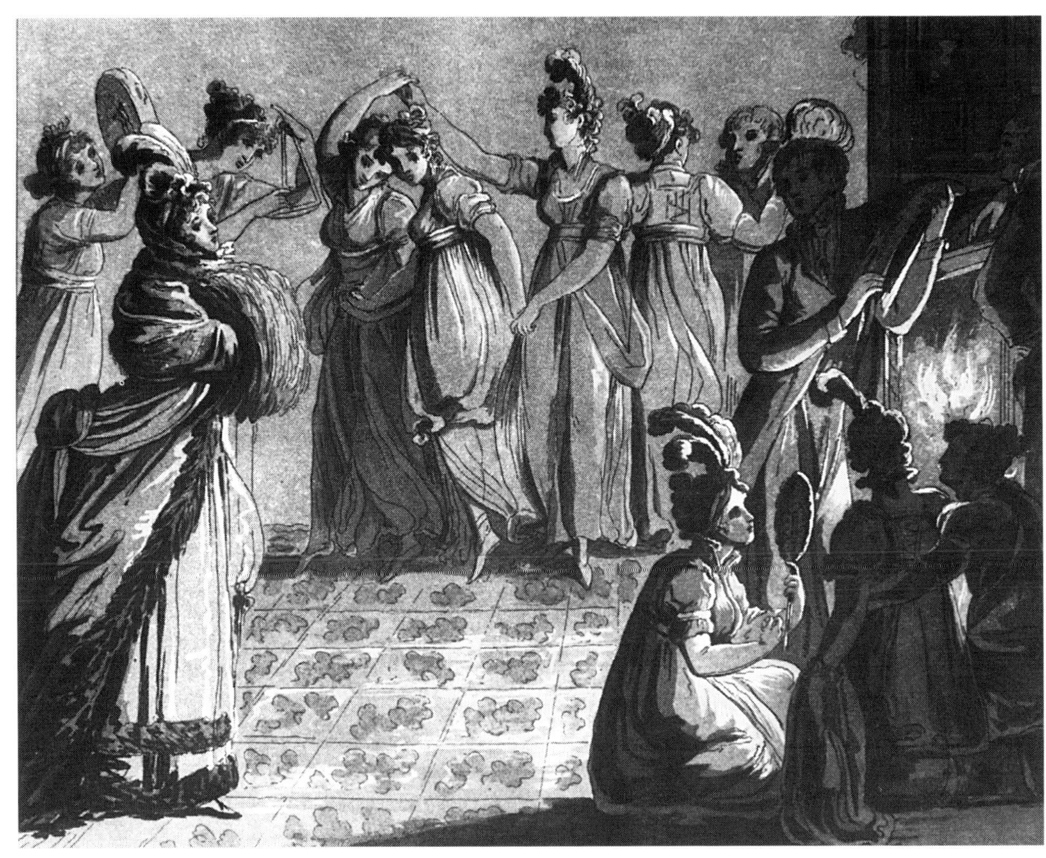

The Winter Day

SECTION III : 38-55 SINGLY ISSUED PRINTS OF NOVELS

38. MARIA
Stipple engraved and published by W. W. Ryland, 12 April 1779, after the painting by Kauffman exhibited at the Royal Academy, 1779, illustrating Sterne's *Sentimental Journey,* of which there is one of several versions at Burleigh House, Stamford.
Lit: Gordon; Kauffman, ill. p.158
380 x 290 (oval 388 x 295)

Sterne's Maria first appeared at the end of *Tristram Shandy,* when Yorick stops his coach on hearing her play vespers on her pipe. Her mind had become unhinged after having 'had her Banns forbid, by the intrigues of the curate of the parish who published them'. In *The Sentimental Journey* Yorick finds her with her dog Sylvio 'sitting with her elbow on her lap, and her head leaning on one side within her hand....afliction had touch'd her looks with something that was scarcely earthly'.

The picture, of which the artist made several repetitions, established itself as one of the most familiar images of the age of sensibility, and was used to decorate objects of all kinds, from ceramics to embroidered fire-screens. Another picture by Kauffman of Sterne and Maria was engraved by J-M.Delattre in 1782 (V & C 1423; ill. Webster p. 68).

William Wynne Ryland (1733-83) was a line engraver who learned stipple engraving in France. In the late 1760s he was established as a print publisher and recognising the appeal of Kauffmann's pictures of the Greek and Roman classics he published several mezzotints after her paintings. He was the first to grasp the new opportunities provided by stipple engraving and with the help of the engraver Thomas Burke he published many successful stipples prior to his conviction for forging two India Bills in 1784. This print is a partially lettered proof, an early impression of the kind which was bought by print collectors and kept in a portfolio.

39. THE DEPARTURE OF LA FLEUR FROM MONTREUIL
Stipple by Thomas Watson, proof before the title, published by Watson and Dickinson, 28 May 1781, after a drawing by Bunbury illustrating Sterne's *Sentimental Journey.*
Lit: George Goodwin, *Thomas Watson,* London, 1904, 70.
410 x 345 (circle 300 diam.)

The handsome valet takes leave of the young women of Montreuil:

> *La Fleur kissed their Hands round and round again, and thrice he wiped his Eyes, and thrice he promised He would bring them all Pardons from Rome.*

Bunbury also drew a set of four very humorous scenes from *Tristram Shandy* which were etched and published by James Bretherton in 1773 (Painted Word Nos. 26-29; P.de Voogd, *The Shandean,* iii, 1991, pp.138-143)

40. LOUISA HAMMOND
Stipple by Bartolozzi, published by Susanna Vivares, 15 September 1781, after a painting by Angelica Kauffman illustrating S. J. Pratt's novel *Emma Corbett, or the Miseries of Civil War,* 1777, Letter XXXIII.
Lit: V&C 1400
(Cut to oval 324 x 260)

This print shows the heroine of a novel 'founded on some events in America'. Samuel Jackson Pratt (1749-1814), is a remarkable Bohemian character included in the *Dictionary of National Biography;* he took orders as a young man, left the church, first worked as an actor and then followed a literary career, sometimes writing under his stage name of Courtenay Melmoth, and producing a long series of plays, travels and poems such as the anonymously issued *Landscapes in Verse. Taken in Spring. By the author of 'Sympathy',* 1783. Although many painters clearly did not need to read literary works in their entirety if there was an established canon of incidents to illustrate, it is likely that Kauffman read

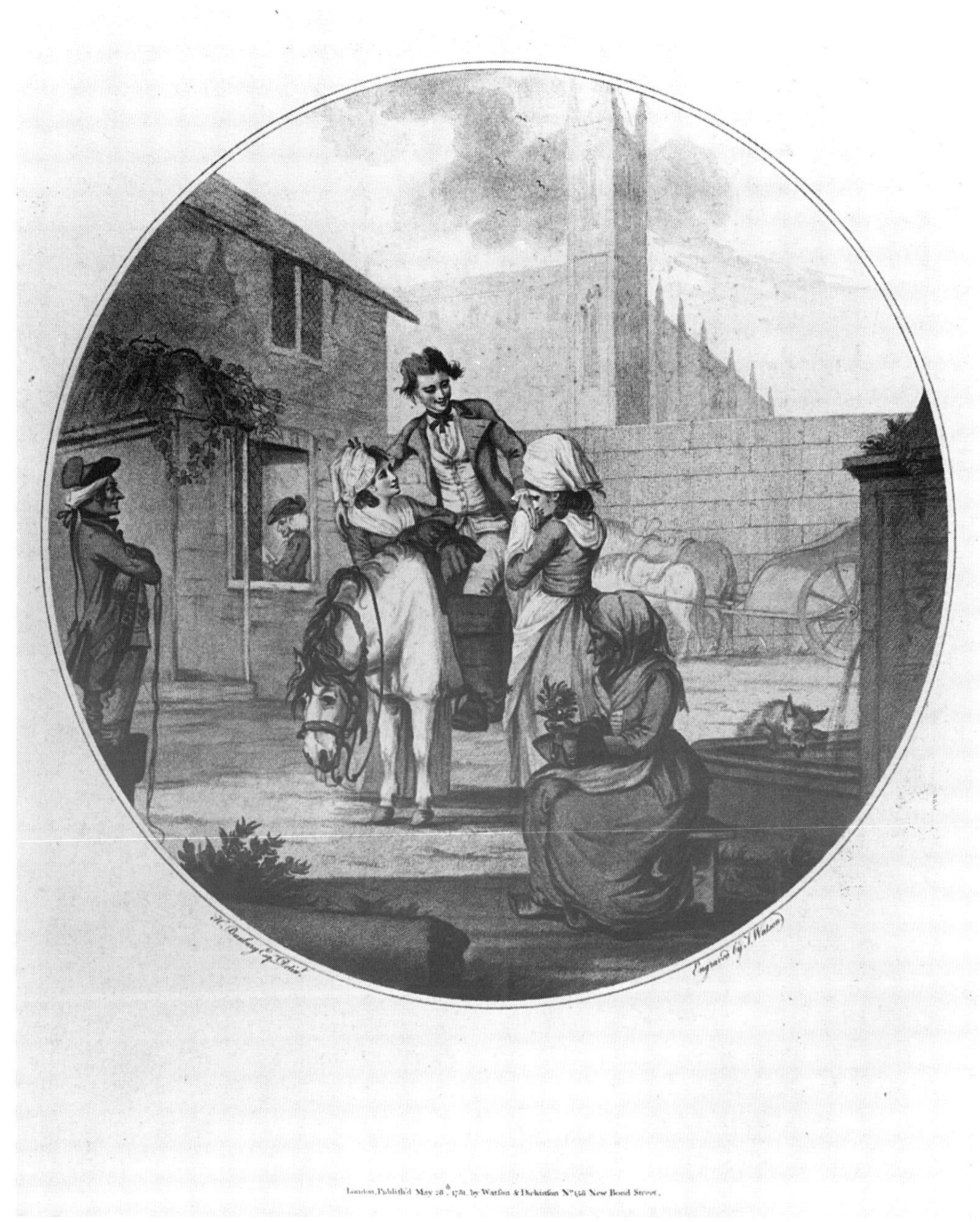

The Departure of La Fleur from Montreuil

his popular novel; a small print after a design by her inspired by the novel was engraved by P.W.Tomkins and published by W.Palmer on 20 December 1781.

Kauffman used the same motif of the seated pensive girl that she employed for Maria. For many buyers of prints such as these the subject matter was irrelevant: it was a decorative design which established a certain mood and which looked good, cut to the engraved oval and framed in gilt. Bartolozzi succeeded Ryland, the engraver of *Maria,* (No. 38) as the leading engraver of Kauffman's pictures.

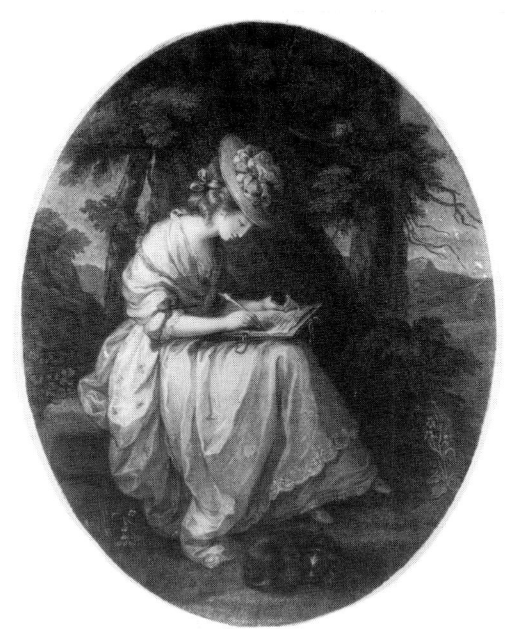

Louisa Hammond

41. ST PREUX AND JULIA
Etching by Francis Wheatley, with engraving by R.Pollard and aquatint by Francis Jukes, published by J.R.Smith, 14 June 1786, after Wheatley's drawing now in the British Museum, to illustrate J.J.Rousseau's *New Eloisa*
Lit: Webster E 5, drawing ill. p. 60.
559 x 413 (510 x 380)

This attractive print is included as a reminder of the importance that continental literature of an affecting kind had both in developing English sensibilities and in providing suitable incidents to depict. St. Preux and Julia are shown at an emotionally charged moment, standing on the edge of a foaming torrent. The watercolour was done shortly after Wheatley had got into financial difficulties in Ireland and, in the words of his Irish friend James Gandon, 'returned to London, where he was eventually compelled to paint and draw for the print-sellers'. This drawing may have been made as a speculation rather than a commission since Wheatley also made some drawings 'intended for publication' after the popular stories of J.F.Marmontel (1723-99) which were sold by auction in 1785. Numerous artists, including Kauffman and P.J. de Loutherbourg illustrated stories by Marmontel such as *The Shepherdess of the Alps.* Other popular works of continental fiction of which there were singly issued plates included Goethe's *The Sorrows of Werther* - the best known of all novels of sentiment, and Madame de Montolieu's *Caroline of Lichtfield,* translated in 1786 (see No. 50).

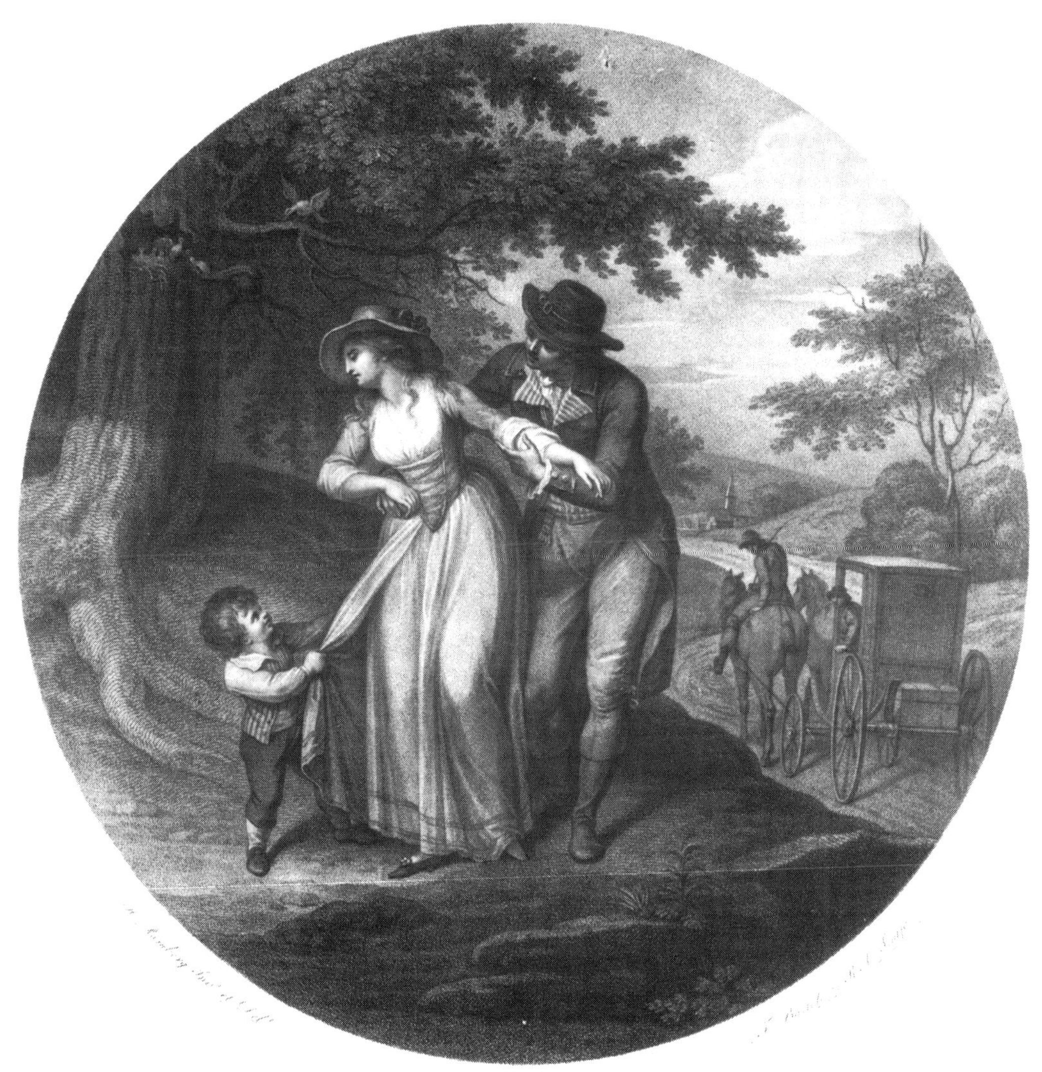

Esq. Thornhill persuades Olivia to elope

42. ESQ. THORNHILL PERSUADES OLIVIA TO ELOPE
43. DOCTOR PRIMROSE FINDS HIS DAUGHTER OLIVIA IN DISTRESS

Pair of stipples by Bartolozzi, published by James Birchall, 1 August 1787, after drawings by Ramberg, illustrating Goldsmith's *Vicar of Wakefield,* 1766.
Lit: Gordon; V&C 1393
(circles 305-8 diam.)

These prints were after drawings which were among several which belonged to - and were probably commissioned by - the printseller James Birchall, an important publisher with a shop in the Strand between about 1778 and his death in 1794. He owned a number of paintings and drawings, notably after Kauffman and Hamilton, who also depicted a number of scenes from English history which Birchall published (Fig. 2).

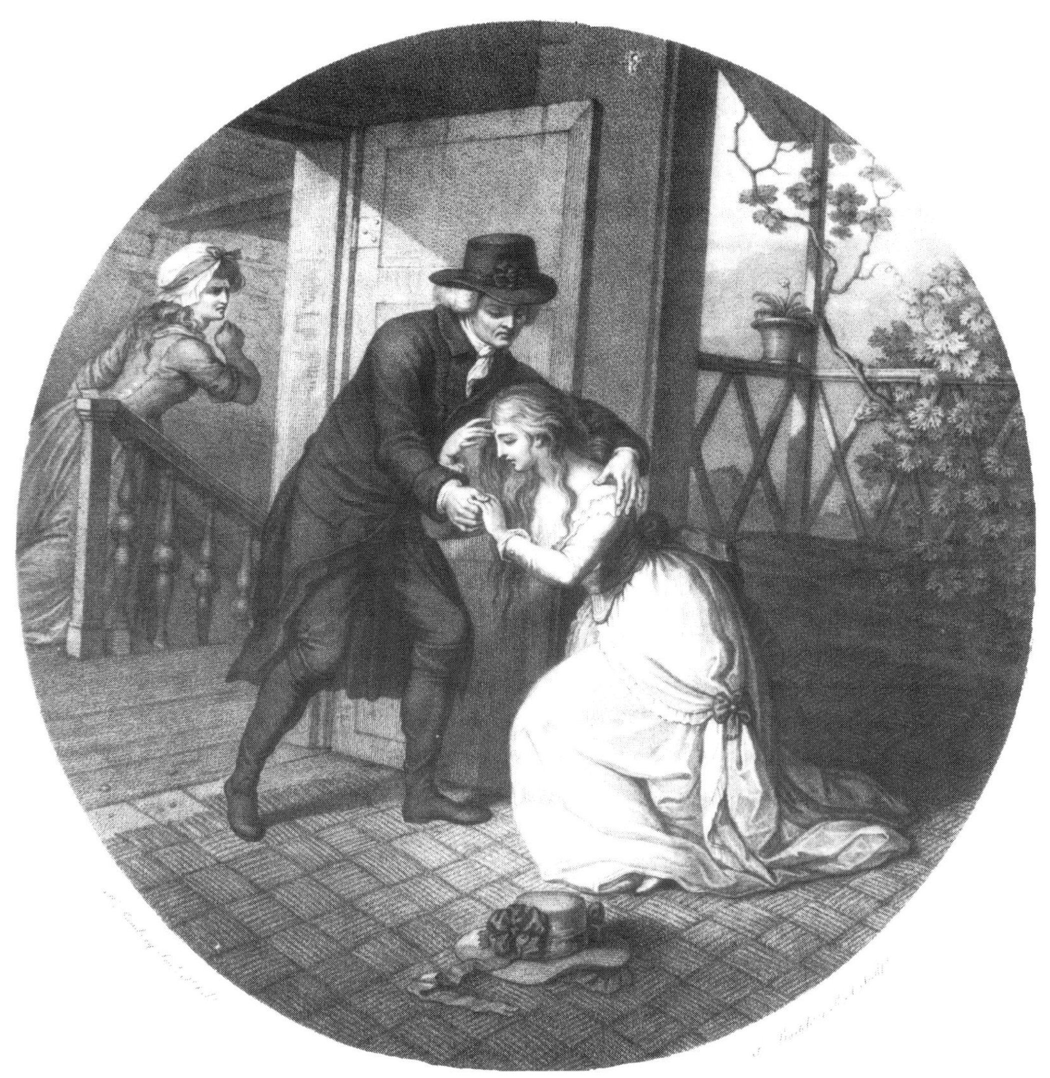

Doctor Primrose finds his daughter Olivia in distress

44. RODERICK RANDOM DISCOVERS HIMSELF TO NARCISSA
One of a pair of stipples by C.Knight, open-letter proof, published by James Birchall, 1 May 1787, after a drawing by Ann Trewingard, illustrating Tobias Smollett's *Roderick Random*, 1748.
(circle 302 diam.)

The name 'Trewingard' is likely to be the lettering engraver's misreading of 'Trewinnard'. The artist is probably the one who exhibited miniatures at the Royal Academy between 1797 and 1806 as Mrs or Miss A or Anna Trewinnard (see also No. 46).

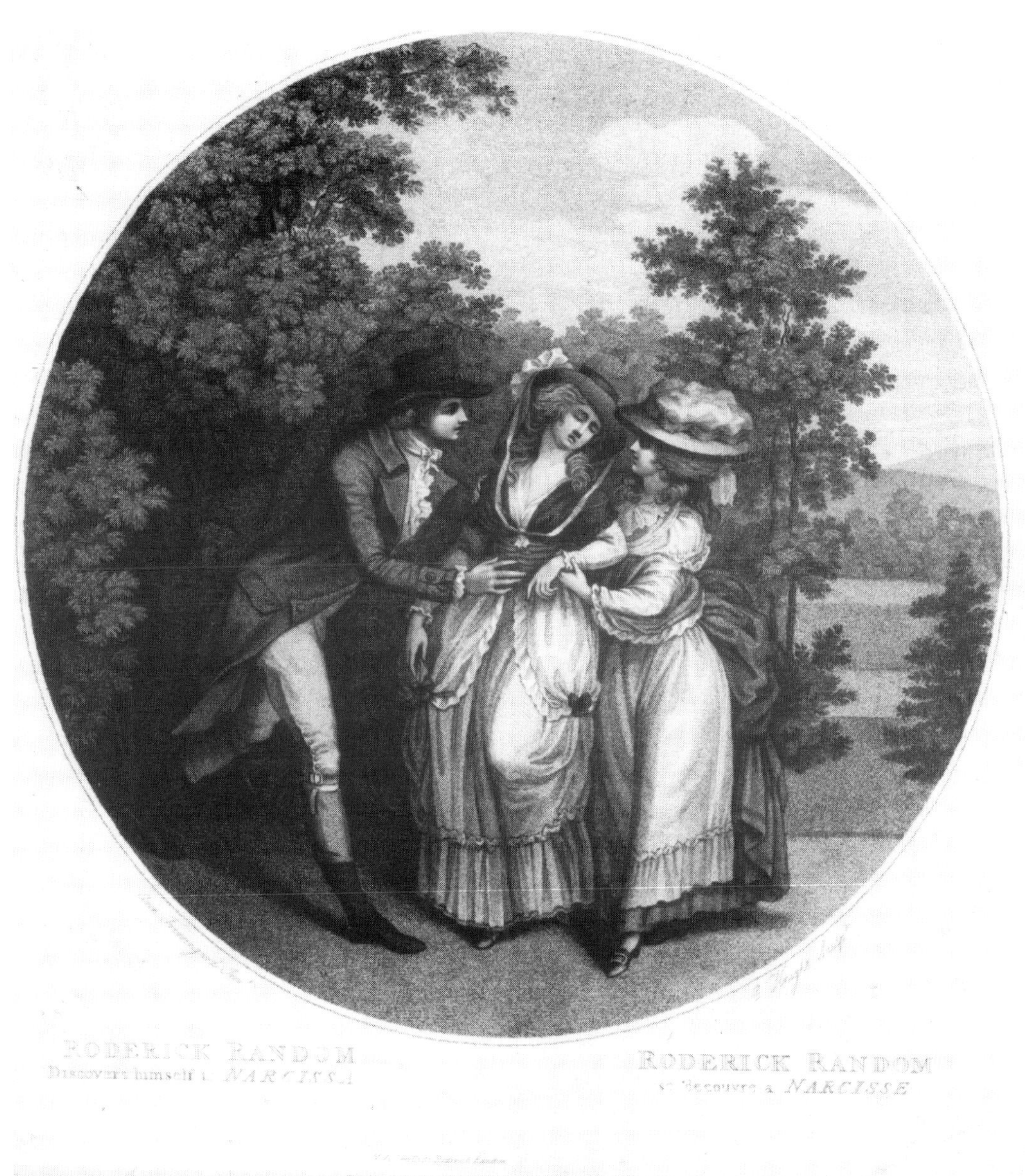

Roderick Random discovers himself to Narcissa

45. OLIVIA'S RETURN TO HER FATHER

Stipple by [C.G.]Playter, one of a pair published by J and J.Boydell, 1 September 1789, after a painting by Stothard illustrating Goldsmith's *Vicar of Wakefield.*
380 x 315 (circle 275 diam.)

The first of this pair shows *Young Thornhill's first Interview with Olivia;* this shows the moment when she is confronted by her mother's sarcasm after she has been brought home by her father.

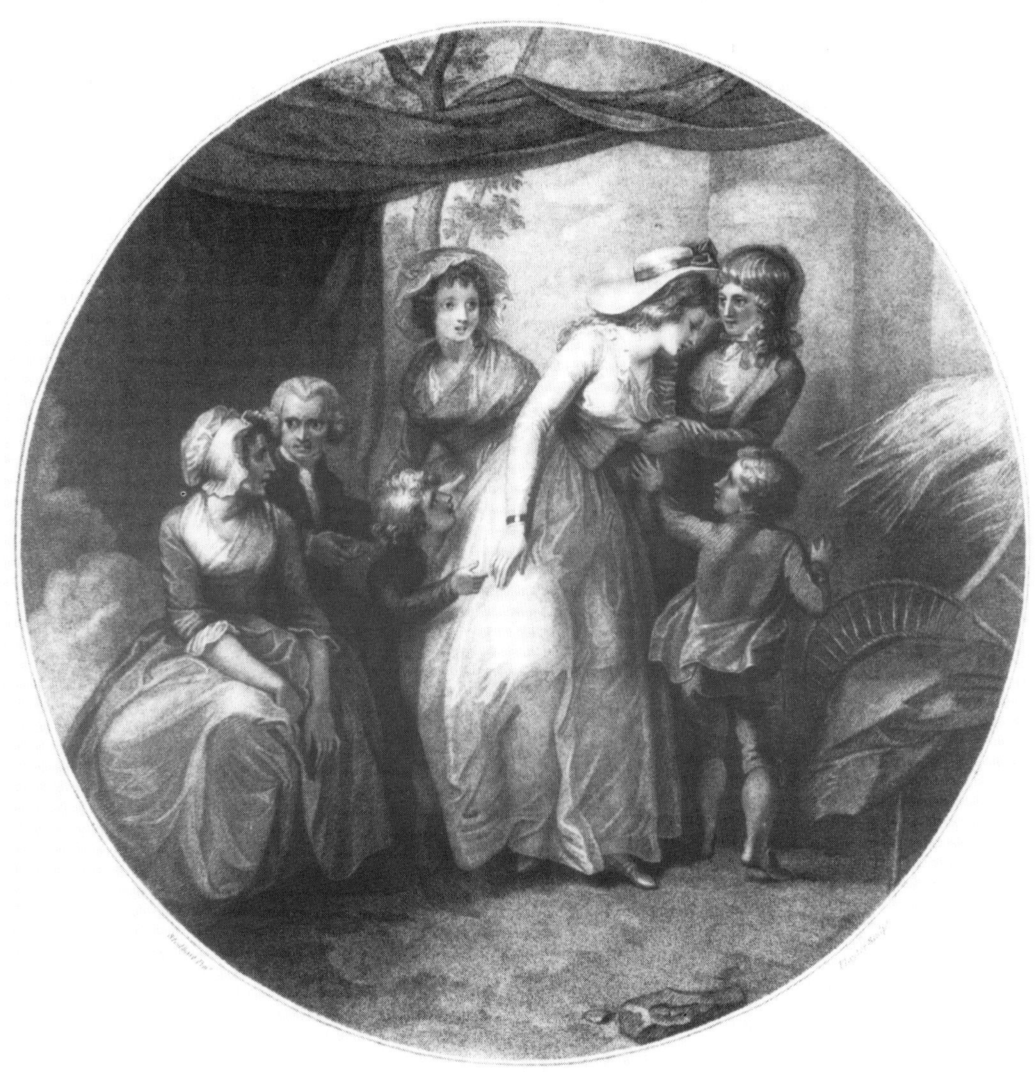

VICAR OF WAKEFIELD.

Olivia's return to her Father.

Olivia's return to her father

By the late 1780s Boydell, who preferred to publish serious prints, was forced by changes in taste to issue more decorative stipples. Over thirty of the sixty plates in the eighth volume of his *Collection of Prints,* which had begun in 1769 with grand line engravings of old master pictures, were stipples, and those with literary connotations included this pair, a pair by Peter Simon of *Tom Jones* after John Downman, a pair of *Camilla* (Nos 47-48) and *Henry and Emma* after Kauffman (No. 21) and its pendant.

46. EVELINA
Stipple by Robert Laurie, publisher unknown. after a drawing by E. Trevaniard, illustrating Fanny Burney's *Evelina*, 1778, Vol. 3d. Page 198.
407 x 350 (circle 300 diam.)

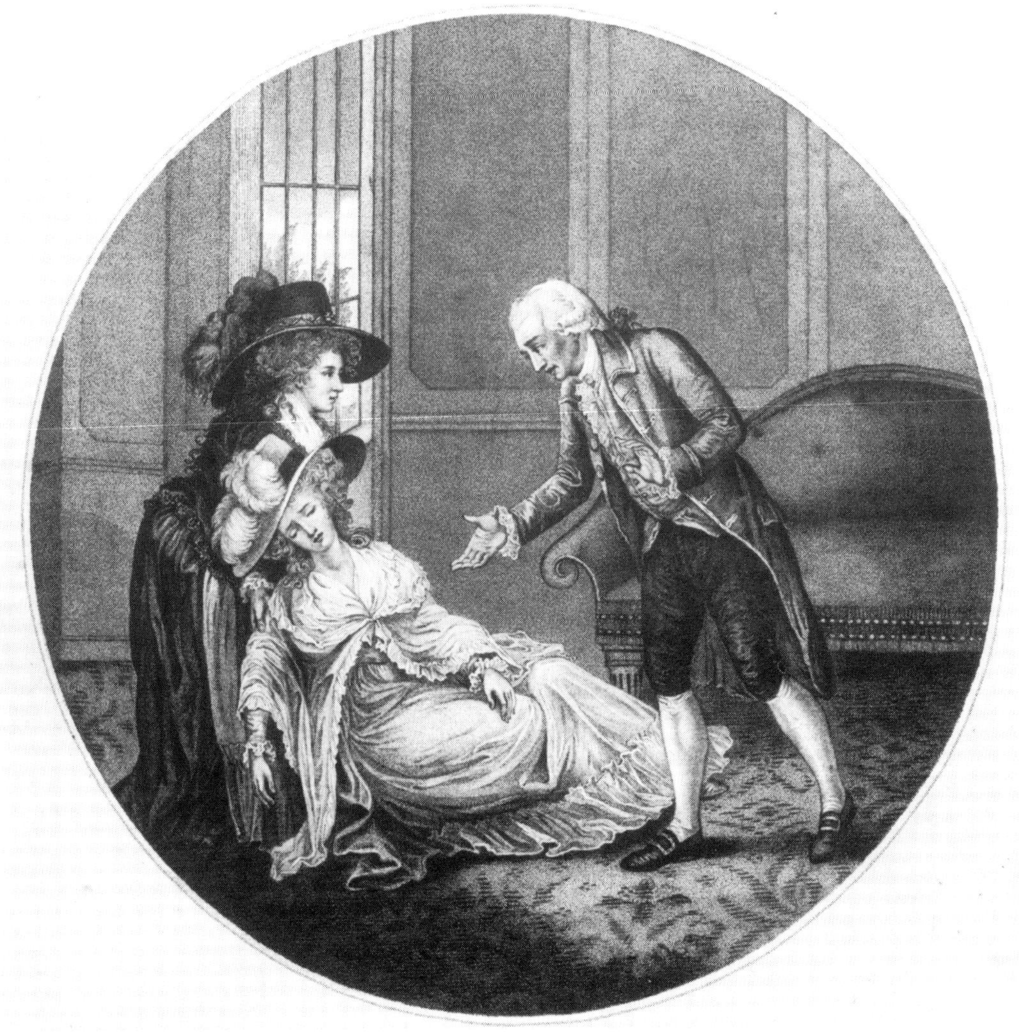

Evelina

This print shows the moment when Sir John Belmont acknowledges the daughter he abandoned as a child: 'Lift up thy head thou image of my long lost Caroline!'. As a result of this she is able to marry the gentlemanly Lord Orville, with whom she is in love.

The name 'Trevaniard' may be the lettering engraver's misreading of 'Trewinnard' (see No. 44)

Robert Laurie (c. 1755-1836) began his career as a mezzotint engraver, and improved methods of printing mezzotints in colours. He later became a successful publisher, trading as Laurie and Whittle.

47. CAMILLA FAINTING IN THE ARMS OF HER FATHER
48. CAMILLA RECOVERING FROM HER SWOON
Pair of stipples by George Keating, published by J & J.Boydell, 1790, after paintings by 'W.Singleton', illustrating Sarah Fielding's *Adventures of David Simple,* 1748.
(subjects c. 280 x 395)

This novel, by the sister of Henry Fielding, describes David Simple's travels 'in the search of a real friend'. These prints show the reconciliation of Camilla, whom he eventually marries, and her father, whose mind has been poisoned against his daughter by his second wife.

The painter is given as 'W.Singleton': William Singleton was a miniature painter and the designer is more likely to have been his pupil and nephew Henry Singleton (1766-1839) who became one of the most prolific painters of subject pictures.

The engraver, George Keating (1762-1842) trained as a mezzotint engraver but also had to turn his hand to stipple; he later became a Catholic bookseller. Boydell sold these prints for 5/- each uncoloured.

49. MRS VINDEX, MEETING WITH MASTER HENRY CLINTON
Stipple by Bartolozzi, one of a pair published by J.F.Tomkins, 1 April 1791, after drawings by P.W.Tomkins, illustrating Henry Brooke's *Fool of Quality,* 1760-72, Vol.III, p.187
Lit: V & C 1402
(oval 215 x 178)

The Fool of Quality, by the Irish writer Henry Brooke (1703-83) was a Rousseauesqe novel, strong in its condemnation of oppression and full of discursive passages. Henry Clinton, the rejected son of an earl who has been brought up by foster-parents, develops into a paragon of manliness, and is constantly relieving the unfortunate; one beneficiary is shown here on her knees thanking him: 'I am the wife of you Vindex, your own Vindex,

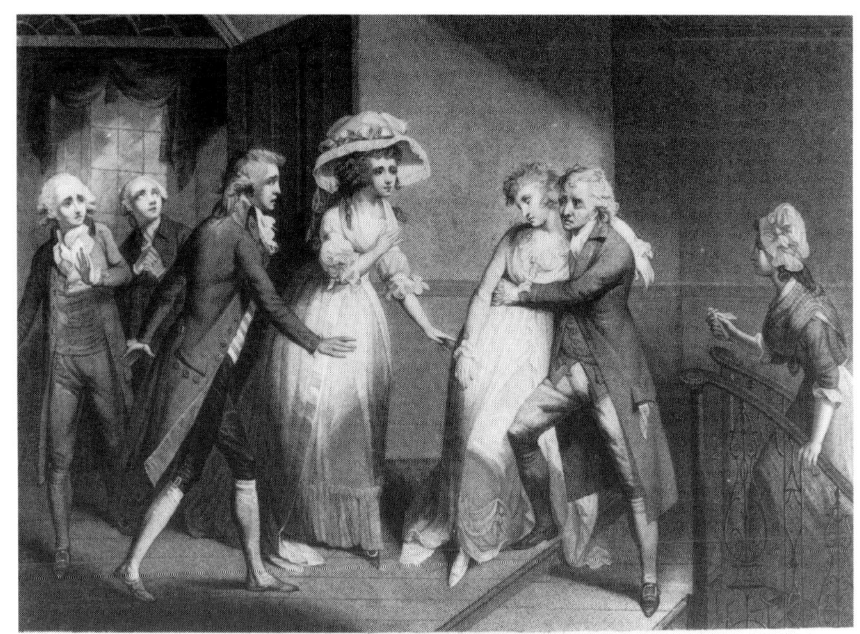

Camilla fainting in the arms of her father

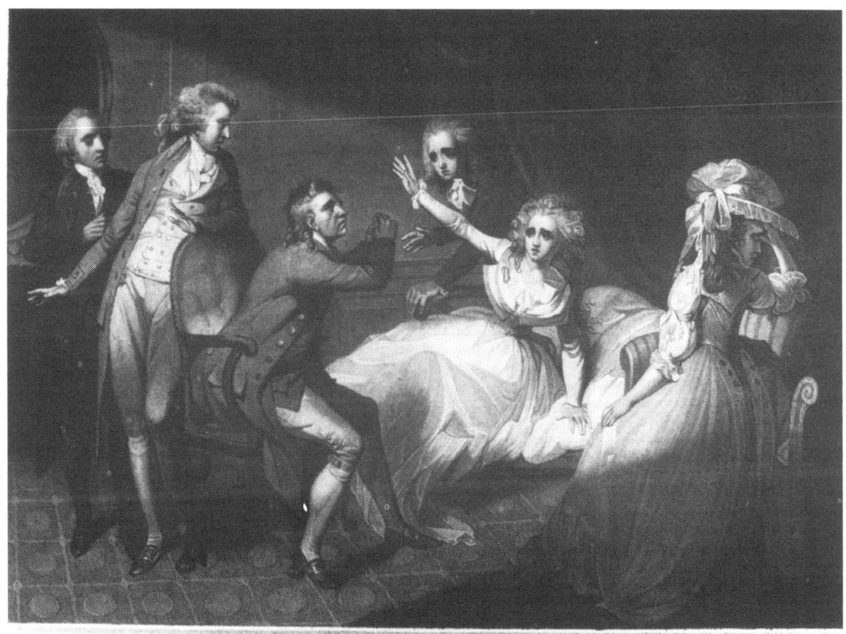

Camilla recovering from her swoon

whom you redeemed from beggary and slavery, whom you restored to his wretched partner, whom you restored to his infant daughter'. The book was much admired by John Wesley who edited it for Methodist use.

Although P.W.Tomkins was best known as a reproductive engraver he also designed a number of prints during his long career. He and his brother, who issued this print, later became prominent print publishers; their best publication was a sumptuous edition dated 1797 of Thomson's *Seasons* with stipples by Peltro and Bartolozzi after paintings by William Hamilton, perhaps the finest book illustrated with stipple engravings; a few copies were issued with the prints printed in colours.

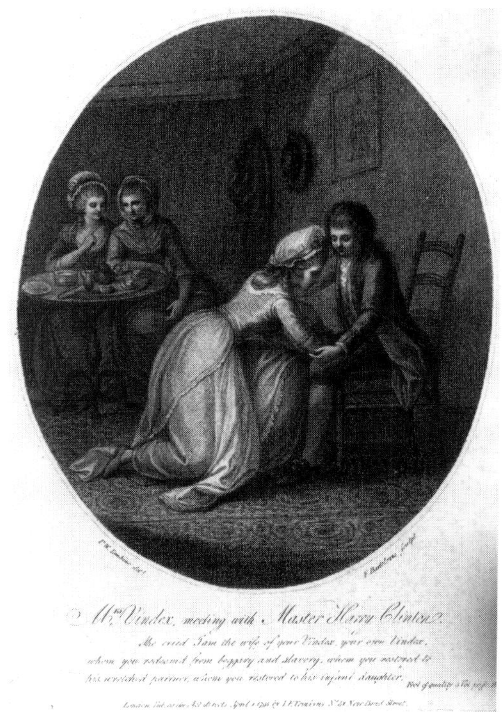

Mrs. Vindex, meeting with Master Henry Clinton

50. CAROLINE OF LICHTFIELD

Colour-printed stipple by Orme, published April 4 1791 by E(lizabeth) Walker & Co., after a painting by Singleton illustrating Elisabeth de Montolieu's *Caroline of Lichtfield* (Subject cut to 350 x 290)

Madame de Montolieu's sentimental novel was enormously successful after its translation from the French by Thomas Holcroft in 1786. The first artist to design singly issued plates based on it was Stothard, whose prints were published in 1787-88. This print illustrates how 'Walsten advanced and saw a young lady at the farther part of the chamber elegantly dressed and tying a black scarf around the neck of a young gentleman so as to support his arm'.

This print was engraved by 'Orme', probably Daniel Orme (1767-post 1832), a miniature painter and engraver who, with his brother Edward, turned in the 1790s to the publication of patriotic prints (Painted Word p. 34).

51. CAPTAIN BOWLING INTRODUCED TO NARCISSA

Hand-coloured aquatint by Thomas Rowlandson, 'Hogarthian Novelist Plate 6' published by C.Lowndes, 1 September 1792, after a drawing by Henry Singleton illustrating Tobias Smollett's *Roderick Random*, 1748, Vol. 2, Chapter 32.

Lit: J.R.Abbey, *Life in England,* 249 (as re-issued by Ackermann 13 May 1800)

280 x 358 (190 x 265)

Roderick Random was the first major novel by Tobias Smollett (1721-71), who had served as a surgeon's mate, a career which he gives to Roderick. His adventures include being taken by smugglers to France where he is able to rescue his uncle Tom Bowling; he falls in love with Narcissa, but nevertheless makes various attempts to marry a fortune. After gambling away his money he serves as a surgeon under his uncle, and meets Don Roderigo, a wealthy trader, who fortunately turns out to be his father; he is then able to return to England and marry Narcissa, whom he is shown here introducing to his uncle.

Thomas Rowlandson (1756-1827) is better known as a draughtsman and etcher of his own drawings than as a reproductive engraver, and he has left his unmistakeable stamp on Singleton's drawing. This print was published by the book publisher C.Lowndes as one of the illustrations to the first of a set of six novels, five by Smollett together with Sterne's *Tristram Shandy,* each of which he planned to issue in six octavo sized parts at the cost of a guinea (£1-1-0) under the title of 'The Hogarthian Novelist'; what was unusual about the venture was that the six prints to be issued with each novel were not intended to be bound up with the completed work: they were advertised as 'neatly coloured, and mounted for framing...on a fine wove paper, hot pressed' (*St. James's Chronicle,* 7-9 August 1792). There were two pairs of plates after drawings by George Woodward and by Singleton and a third pair after Samuel Collings engraved by J.C.Stadler. It is interesting that Lowndes should have made an appeal to the name of Hogarth; perhaps it was to emphasise the robustness of the works, in contrast to the pallidness of so much fiction of the time. The venture does not seem to have prospered as he did not bring out the other volumes. The six plates were acquired by Ackermann who advertised the set in his catalogue of 1802 at 6/- plain or 10/6d coloured.

52. CECILIA

Stipple by F.Masetti, published by A.Suntach, 1795, after another print of a painting by Thomas Stothard illustrating Fanny Burney's novel *Cecilia, or Memoirs of an Heiress,* 1782, Book III, Chapter 3.
(oval 245 x 310)

The mad but moral soothsayer, Mr Albany, introduces the heiress Cecilia to Henrietta as an appropriate recipient of her charity. A friendship between the two women follows, and misinterpretations of Cecilia's dealings with Henrietta's family act as catalysts to the development of the plot.

This print is a pirated copy of an English print, and is in reverse to the original. Antonio Suntach (1744-1828) was born in Venice but worked in Bassano for the famous firm of Remondini, who sent their cheap copies of prints all over Europe, before setting up a similar enterprise. The print carries a French translation of the relevant passage from the novel. Suntach's prints were usually of a higher quality than other Italian piracies.

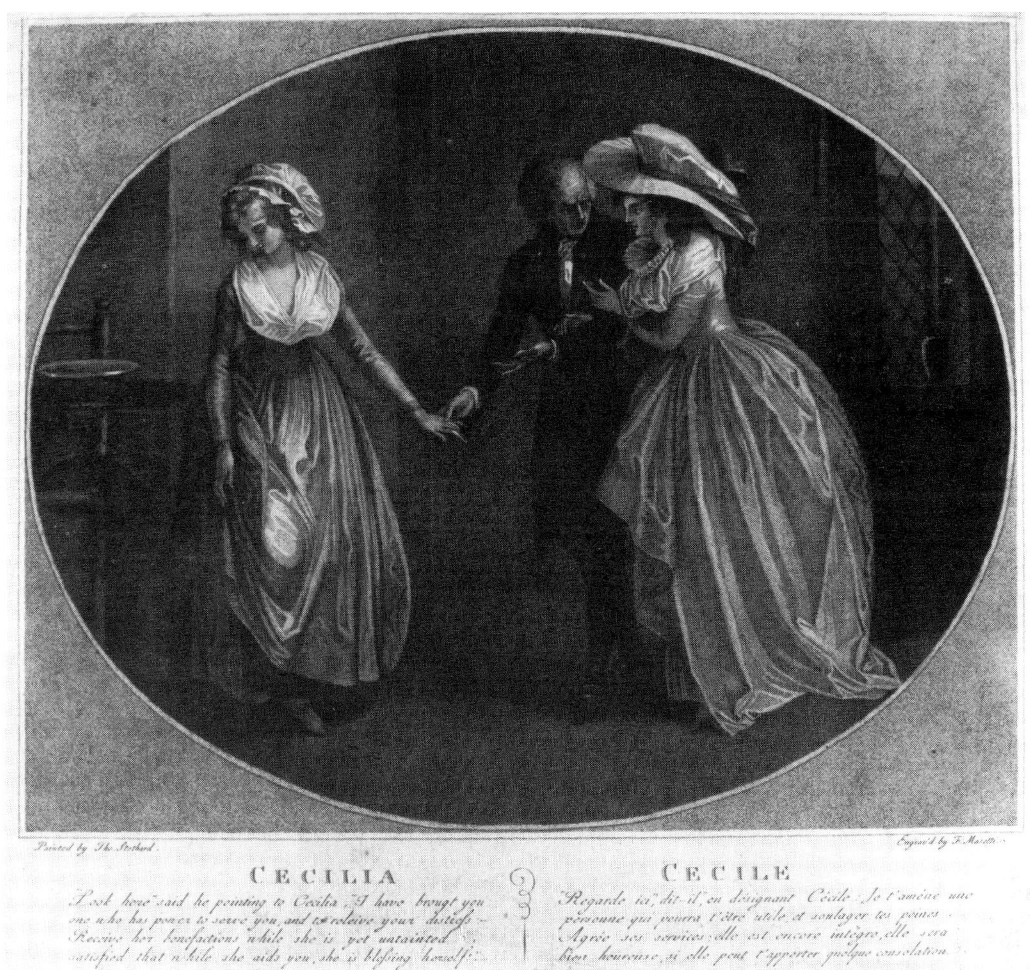

Cecilia

53-54. THE RECESS

Pair of stipples, partially printed in colours with additional hand-colouring, engraved and published by John Goldar, 15 June 1795, after drawings by Henry Richter exhibited at the Royal Academy, one in 1789 and the other in 1790, illustrating Sophia Lee's *The Recess, or a Tale of Other Times,* 1785.

c. 343 x 405 (ovals 255 x 318)

This gothick novel is set in Elizabethan times and tells the gloriously improbable story of the twin children of Mary Queen of Scots who were concealed for their safety in the 'Recess'. In the first print Leicester makes himself known to the girls, while in the second, one twin is shown reproaching Queen Elizabeth for her treatment of Essex - the favourite who plotted against her and was executed - while the other twin comforts the Queen.

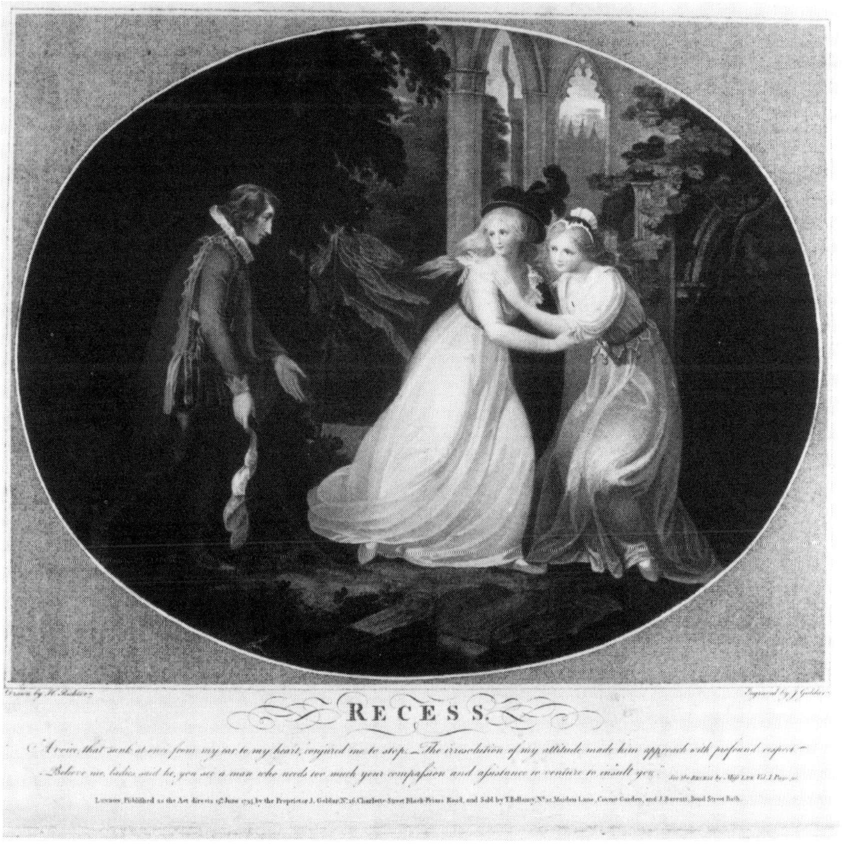

Recess

John Goldar (1729-95) was primarily a line engraver, known for prints after humorous artists such as John Collett; these prints show him turning, right at the end of his career, to the market for fashionable stipples. The publication line indicates that the prints were also sold by J.Barratt in Bond Street, Bath, that well-known haunt of novel readers, as well as in London.

55. THE MYSTERIES OF UDOLPHO

Colour-printed stipple, engraved and published by William Bond, 1796, after a painting by Henry Singleton illustrating Ann Radclffe's novel *The Mysteries of Udolpho,* 1794, vol. ii, chapter 10.
(subject 505 x 405)

The orphaned Emily de St Aubert, in love with the well-born but poor Valancourt, is removed by her aunt to the gloomy castle of Udolpho in the Appenines where her sinister husband Signor Montoni carries on his secret activities. This print shows Montoni ordering his wife to be taken away, with Emily - on the point of fainting - seated in the

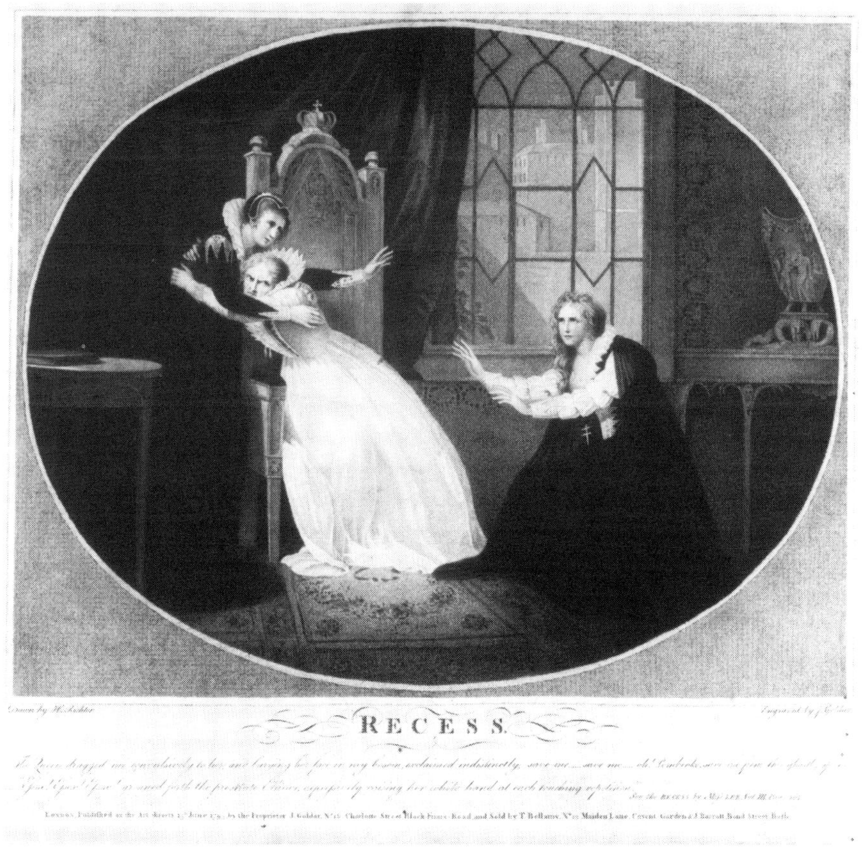

Recess

centre. Emily escapes and meets Valancourt, while Montoni turns out to be the head of a group of bandits and is finally brought to justice. This gothick novel, whose copyright brought Mrs Radcliffe (1764-1823) the large sum of £500, was an enormous success, with its combination of fascinating Latin rogues, suspense, terror and vulnerable females. It is significant that this episode should have been painted and a large print such as this issued within two years of the novel's appearance. In 1797 Singleton exhibited a picture 'from the Mysteries of Udolpho' at the Royal Academy which is probably this picture.

William Bond (1762-1828 or after) was a highly regarded stipple engraver, who continued to engrave portraits for publishers in stipple to the end of his career.

The print is in its original gilded neo-classical frame of flat section with lambs' tongue sight moulding, drummed onto a stretcher as if it were an oil painting; gummed on the back of the print is the label of 'W & J Staveley, Carvers, Gilders & Frame Makers, Stonegate, York' engraved by 'Harrison York' (Fig. 5). The partnership of William and James was dissolved in 1809 (for an earlier card of theirs see T.Friedman, *Engrav'd Cards of Tradesmen...in Yorkshire*, exhibition catalogue, Temple Newsam House, Leeds, 1976, No. 17). 'Harrison' is presumably the York engraver John Harrison (1763-1830).

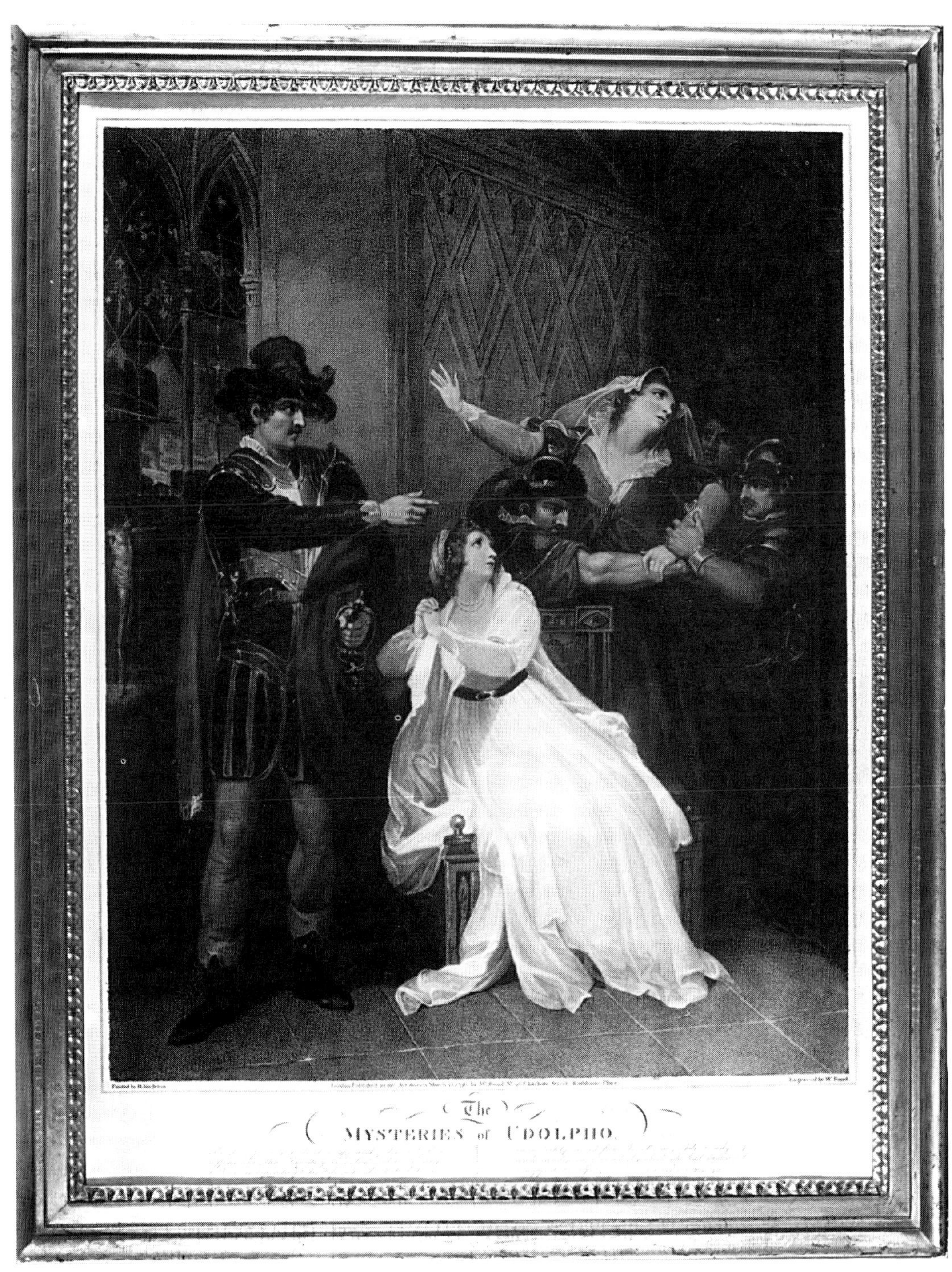

The Mysteries of Udolpho

SECTION IV : 56-65 PRINTS OF SHAKESPEARE'S PLAYS

56. MIRANDA
Stipple by Caroline Watson, published by R. E.Pine, 1782, after his painting of *The Tempest,* Act I, as re-issued by Boydell, 1 June 1784
380 x 450 (330 x 430)

This print shows Miranda's first sight of Ferdinand; it was one of the first pair of a set of pictures announced by Robert Edge Pine (1742-90) in 1781 and exhibited the following year in the Great Room in Spring Gardens. The venture did not, in the words of the contemporary painter Edward Edwards, 'answer to his expectations'. Pine left for America in 1784, taking many of his pictures with him but selling his copper plates to Boydell. Pine, son of the engraver John Pine who had cooperated with William Hogarth in lobbying for the Engravers' Copyright Act of 1735, was a man of radical views and it is worth noting that he dedicated the print to the famous Georgiana, Duchess of Devonshire (1757-1806), an ardent supporter of the Whig politician Charles James Fox.

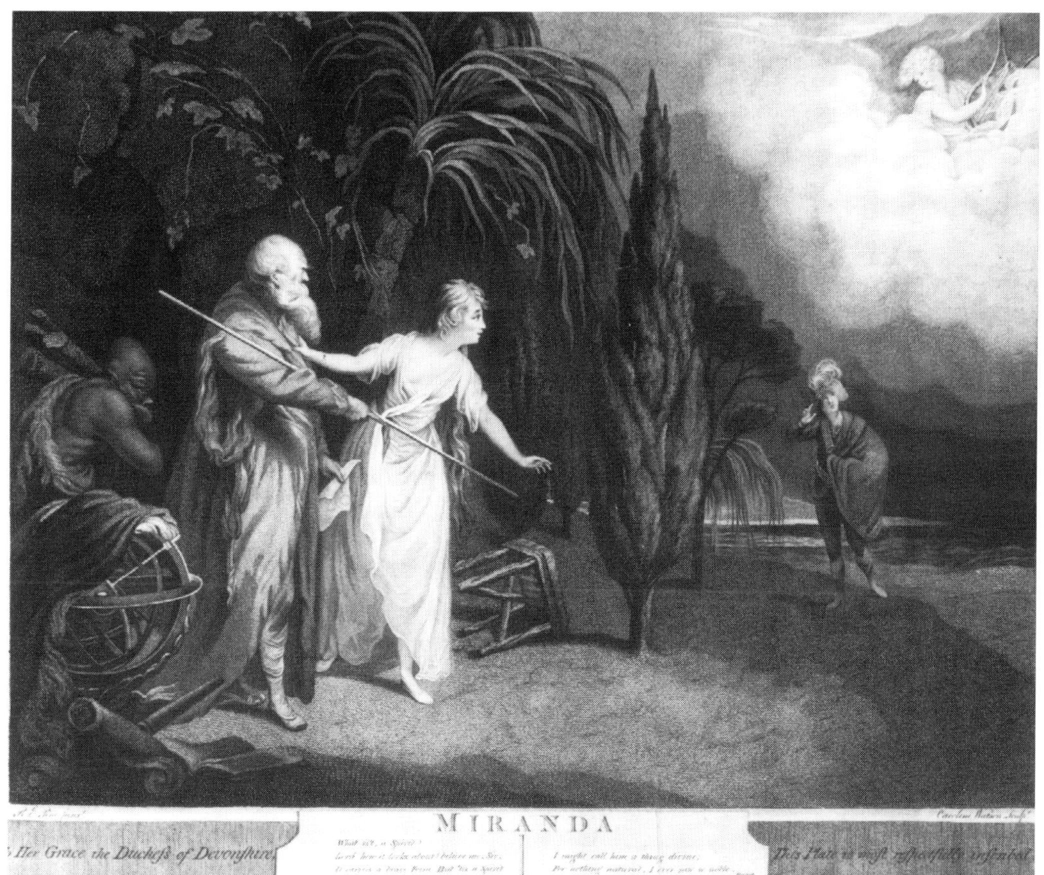

Miranda

57. FALSTAFF AND DOLL TEARSHEET

Colour-printed stipple engraved and published by William Flaxman, 10 March 1783, after a drawing by John Flaxman, illustrating *Henry IV, Part 2,* Act II.
(circle 135 diam.)

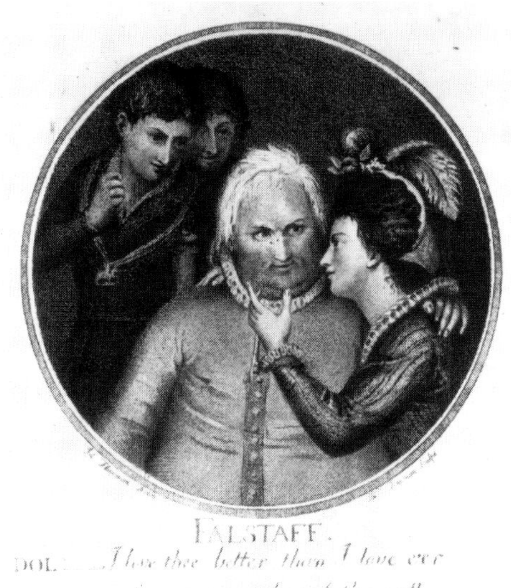

Falstaff and Doll tearsheet

This print, showing Doll saying to Falstaff 'I love thee better than I love e'er a scurvy young boy of them all', is interesting as being designed by the sculptor John Flaxman (1755-1826) prior to his journey to Rome and engraved by his brother William. There was a new interest in the figure of Falstaff following the publication in 1777 of Maurice Morgann's *Essay on the Dramatic Character of Sir John Falstaff.* This was not the only literary stipple which John Flaxman designed; he also made a drawing of *Edward and Angelina,* from the ballad in Goldsmith's *Vicar of Wakefield,* which was engraved by Marcuard and published by Durand, 1 March 1783.

58. MARGARET OF ANJOU

Colour-printed stipple by Charles White, published by Macklin, 20 January 1784, after a drawing by Stothard illustrating *Henry VI*, now at the Courtauld Institute, London.
380 x 330 .(circle 300 diam.)

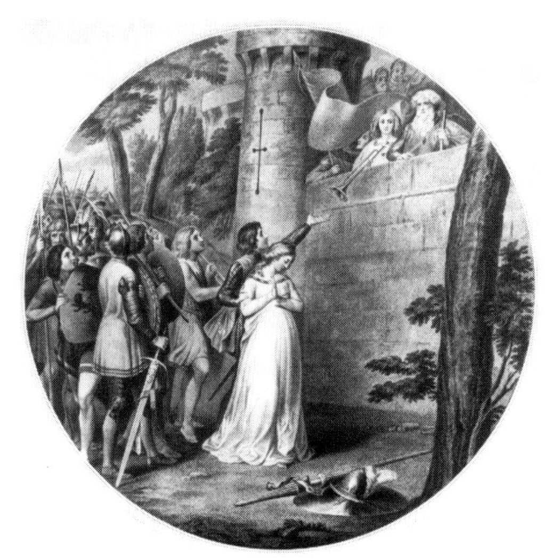

Margaret of Anjou

Stothard was best at scenes of a domestic kind, such as No. 45; this is one of his less convincing designs, but it indicates the interest in Shakespeare, subsequently obscured by Boydell's effective publicity, which preceded the launching of his *Shakespeare.* This is one of at least three singly issued plates after Shakespearian scenes by Stothard which Macklin published in the early 1780s; others were *Ophelia,* by Ogborne, published 25

October 1783 and *Lear and Cordelia,* by Delattre, published 10 September 1784; he issued others after W.Harding. Stothard also provided seven drawings for the Taylors' *Picturesque Beauties of Shakespeare,* a set of line engravings issued in parts between 1783 and 1787.

Charles White (1751-85) was a stipple engraver who is notable for the large number of decorative stipples which he engraved after designs by fashionable ladies such as Countess Spencer, the Countess of Lincoln and Emma Crewe.

59-63 BOYDELL'S *SHAKESPEARE*

59. THE MURDER OF THE PRINCES IN THE TOWER

Line engraving by Francis Legat, published by Boydell, 1790, after the painting by James Northcote, illustrating *King Richard III,* Act IV, Scene 3, exhibited at the Royal Academy in 1786 and now at Petworth House, Sussex.
Lit: Painted Word No. 49.
570 x 415 (500 x 372)

James Northcote (1746-1831) studied under Reynolds and determined to become a history painter. He spent three years in Italy where he was influenced by Fuseli, returning to London in 1780. His subject pictures soon began to be engraved but he still aimed to paint history pictures. The favourable public reception given to this picture encouraged Boydell, who purchased it for 40 guineas, to launch the 'Shakespeare Gallery', for which Northcote painted nine pictures. In his old age Northcote said that

> it was a noble undertaking....but I never thought it could succeed here..
> I knew it must prove his ruin...it was such a collection of slip-slop
> imbecility as was dreadful to look at, and turned out, as I expected it
> would, in the ruin of poor Boydell's affairs... I was indeed sorry that it
> turned out so badly, for it enabled me to become an historical painter...
> (ed. E.Fletcher, *Conversations of James Northcote*, London 1901, pp.113-114)

Northcote tried to emulate Hogarth by painting and publishing in 1797 a set of ten large stipples by Gaugain of narrative pictures entitled *Diligence and Dissipation;* these showed the contrasting careers of two servant girls, but the pictures lacked charm and the venture did not succeed.

Francis Legat (1755-1809) trained in Edinburgh but the openings for line engravers there were limited and he went to London in 1780, being principally employed by Boydell; his line engravings for the Boydell *Shakespeare* were admired and stood out against the blandness of the stipple in which the majority of the plates were engraved.

60. HERO AND URSULA, WITH BEATRICE LISTENING, IN THE GARDEN
Colour-printed stipple by Peter Simon, published by Boydell, 1790, after the painting by the Rev. M.W. Peters, illustrating *Much Ado About Nothing,* Act III, Scene 1, recently in the Northbrook Collection
(subject 562 x 406)

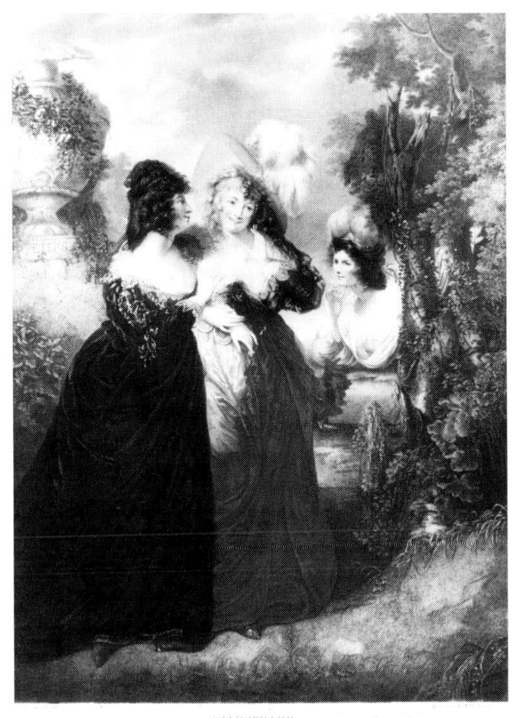

Hero and Ursula, with Beatrice listening, in the garden

Matthew William Peters (1741/2-1814) worked as a portrait and genre painter and painted a number of suggestive pictures of women, many of which were engraved. He became a full member of the Royal Academy in 1777 but was ordained in the early 1780s; he gained preferment in the Church and gave up painting, but took up his brushes to assist Boydell - a move for which he received some criticism. His rejoinder was that he could 'see no more harm in painting Shakespeare than for Bishop Warburton to comment him'. His pictures for the Gallery were among the few which were thoroughly popular; whereas many of the Boydell pictures were destroyed in the nineteenth century this picture is one of those which survived.

The engraver John Peter Simon was almost continuously in Boydell's employ.

61. THE ENCHANTED ISLAND BEFORE THE CELL OF PROSPERO
Stipple by Peter Simon, published by Boydell, 29 September 1797, after the painting by Henry Fuseli, illustrating *The Tempest,* Act I, Scene 2, of which a fragment with the figure of Prospero is in York City Art Gallery.
Lit: Schiff 742; Weinglass
495 x 630 (437 x 585)

Given Fuseli's earlier interest in painting Shakespearian scenes it is not surprising that he should have reacted with enthusiasm to Boydell's scheme, writing in 1788 that it was 'a nursery of historic painting, as a hint towards the true method of calling forth the grandeur of art in a country whose religion, climate and fashions have hitherto repressed it'. This picture was exhibited at the Gallery in 1789, the year in which it was opened with thirty four pictures. Eight paintings by Fuseli were engraved in the large format and he was the most important single contributor.

62. HENRY V SURPRISING CAMBRIDGE, SCROPE AND GREY WITH THEIR DEATH SENTENCE
Stipple by Robert Thew, etched proof dated 1789 of the print published by Boydell, 1798, after the painting by Fuseli, illustrating *Henry V*, Act II, Scene 2.
Lit: Schiff 725; Weinglass
(subject 440 x 593)

This chilling incident provided exactly the kind of dramatic scene which Fuseli relished. This impression is a proof, showing the preliminary etching. Such impressions were printed to show the engraver how the plate was progressing; in turn the engraver or publisher frequently showed progress proofs to the painter who might 'touch' them to indicate changes he wanted - a procedure often dreaded by engravers since the changes which took seconds to draw could entail weeks of work on the copper plate. Nine years passed between the production of this proof and the publication of the final lettered state, though the engraver had probably finished the plate well before 1798. Early proofs were also shown to potential subscribers and were sought after by some print collectors.

Robert Thew (1758-1802), son of a Holderness publican was largely self-taught as an engraver. After serving as a soldier he set up as an engraver in Hull in 1783, but had such ability that he soon moved to London and engraved no less than nineteen of the large *Shakespeare* plates.

63. TROILUS AND CRESSIDA
Stipple by L.Schiavonetti, published by J.& J.Boydell 1795, after a painting by Kauffman illustrating *Troilus and Cressida,* Act V, Scene II.
505 x 630 (443 x 587)

Kauffman was commissioned by Boydell to paint two pictures which she sent from Rome. This picture is a rather disappointing effort and the print shows how uninteresting stipple could be on a large scale.

64. PRINCE ARTHUR BEGS HUBERT FOR HIS SIGHT
Line engraving by John Hall, published by James Woodmason, 1794, after the painting by John Opie illustrating *King John,* Act IV, Scene 1.
Lit: Robin Hamlyn, 'An Irish Shakespeare Gallery', *Burlington Magazine,* cxx, 1978, pp. 515-529.
380 x 280 (245 x 200)

In 1793 James Woodmason, a Dublin-based stationer, opened a 'Shakespeare Gallery' on Boydell's lines in Dublin; for this he commissioned pictures, not from Irish artists, but from many of the painters employed by Boydell, notably Peters, Fuseli and William Hamilton. His enterprise was not well received and after a single season he moved the pictures to a 'New Shakespeare Gallery' in premises near Boydell's in Pall Mall; this lasted only a few months, but a number of prints of the pictures did appear.

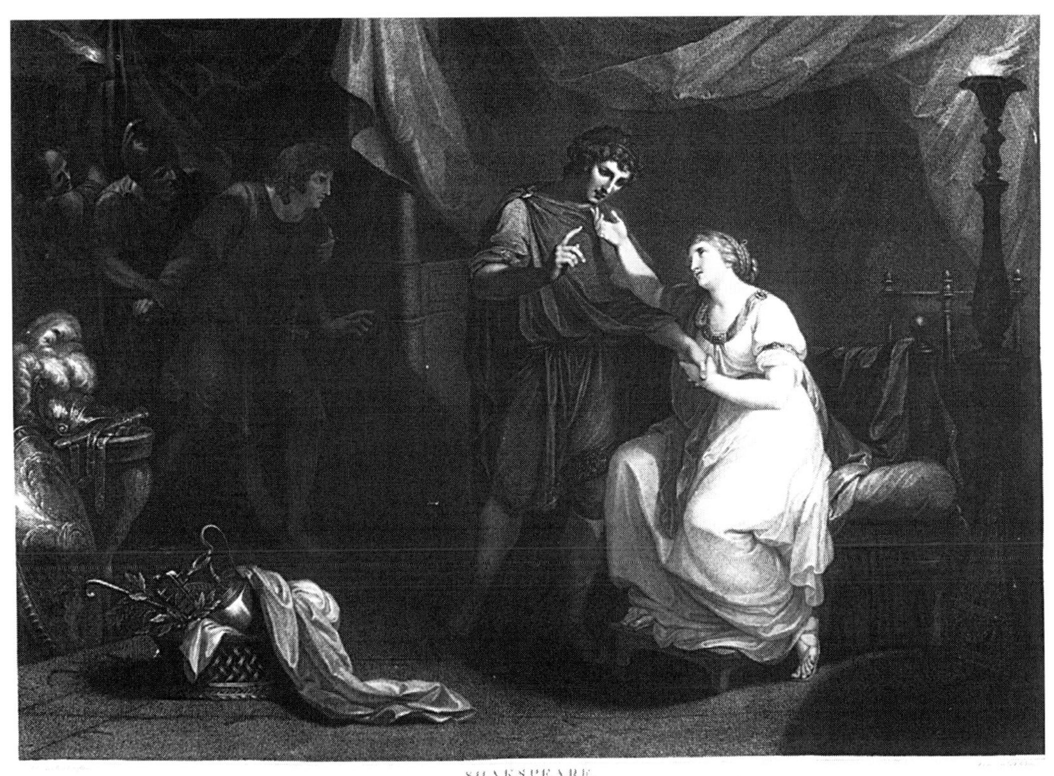

Troilus and Cressida

John Hall (1739-97) was a distinguished line engraver, best known for his engravings after Benjamin West's historical pictures. He was never tempted away from line engraving to work in stipple; he and his assistants did however engrave a great many book illustrations and were not confined to work only on large plates, which could be long and unremunerative.

65. LAUNCE TEACHING HIS DOG CRAB TO BEHAVE AS A DOG IN ALL THINGS
Colour-printed stipple, unsigned, published by Macklin, 1794, after a drawing by Henry Bunbury illustrating *The Two Gentlemen of Verona,* Act IV, Scene 4.
415 x 475 (350 x 445)

This amusing print comes from a set of Shakespearian illustrations commissioned by Macklin from Henry Bunbury, who drew a number of the most endearing dogs. This venture was given the support of the Duchess of York, who owned the drawing for this print.

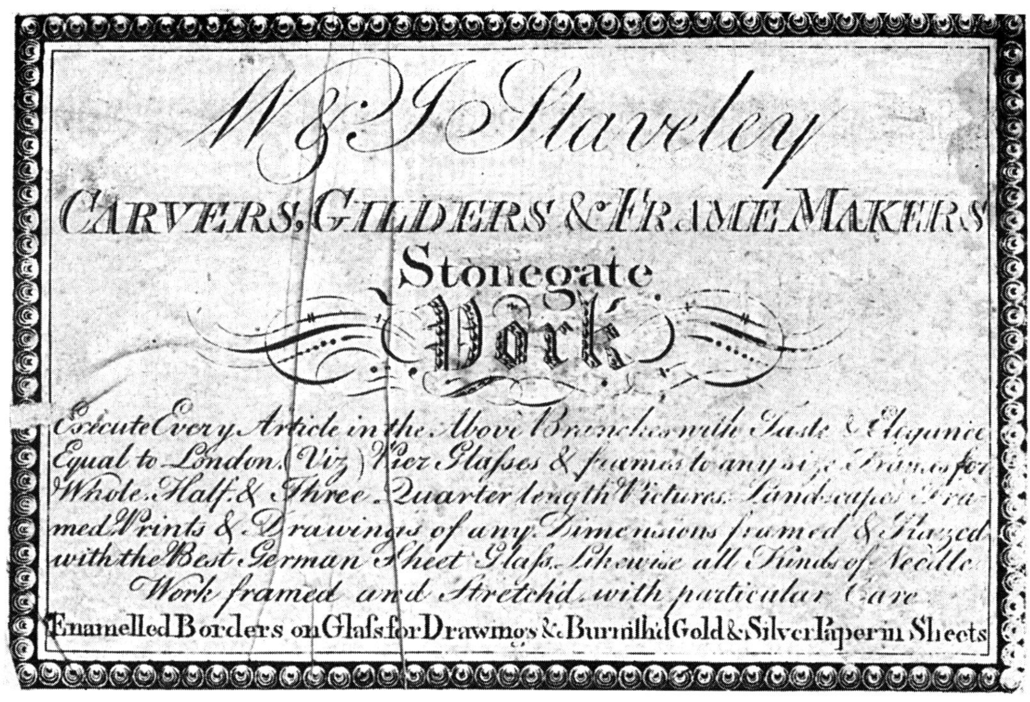

Fig 5

A NOTE ON FRAMES

Appropriate framing is important if late eighteenth century plates are to be seen as they were intended. Prints were generally close framed and many stipples were cut to their oval or circular subject areas, with their titles pasted onto the back of the frame. The prints in this exhibition are shown in a variety of frames, including ones made of pine, veneered fruitwood, pressed metal and various patterns of gilt. Some notes on the frames have been added to the exhibition labels but this information is not relevant to the purpose of this catalogue and is therefore not repeated here (an exception has been made for the frame of No. 55 and its interesting trade label, Fig. 5). Two articles may be recommended to those interested in the subject:

Joan D.Dolmetsh, 'Colonial America's Elegantly Framed Prints', *The Magazine Antiques,* May 1981, pp. 1106-1112

Pippa Mason, Framing Prints in England 1640-1820, *Museum Management* and *Curatorship,* 11, 1992, pp. 117-132.

ABBREVIATIONS AND BIBLIOGRAPHY

This bibliography lists some of the general works which contain information about the artistic background and to which reference has been made in the text:

Altick	Altick, Richard.D, *Paintings from Books: Art and Literature in Britain, 1760-1900,* Columbus,Ohio, 1985. (This book is a remarkable achievement, but understandably concentrates on major writers and painters).
Coxhead	A.C.Coxhead, *Thomas Stothard, R.A.*, London, 1906
Frankau	Julia Frankau, *John Raphael Smith,* London, 1902
Gordon	C.M.Gordon, *British Painting of Subjects from the English Novel, 1740-1870*, Ph.D. thesis, New York, 1988.
Hammelmann	Hanns Hammelmann, edited and completed by T.S.R.Boase, *Book Illustrators in Eighteenth Century England,* New Haven and London, 1975
Kauffman	ed. Wendy W.Roworth, *Angelica Kauffman: A Continental Artist in Georgian England,* London, 1992.
Painted Word	ed. Peter Cannon-Brookes, *The Painted Word: British History Painting: 1750-1830,* Woodbridge, 1991.
Pointon	Marcia Pointon, *Milton and English Art,* Manchester, 1970.
Schiff	Gert Schiff, *Johann Heinrich Fussli,* 2 vols, Zurich, 1973.
V & C	A.de Vesme and A.Calabi, *Francesco Bartolozzi,* Milan, 1928.
Weinglass	David H.Weinglass, *Engraved Illustrations By and After Henry Fuseli: A Catalogue Raisonné,* Aldershot, 1993.

INDEX BY CATALOGUE ENTRY

INDEX OF AUTHORS

INDEX OF DESIGNERS

INDEX BY CATALOGUE ENTRY

INDEX OF ENGRAVERS

INDEX OF PUBLISHERS